Club PROGRAMS for Teens

100 activities for the entire year

Amy J. Alessio and Heather Booth

ala editions

An imprint of the American Library Association
Chicago   2015

D1376771

AMY J. ALESSIO has enjoyed the input of teens for over nineteen years as an award-winning teen librarian at the Schaumburg Township District Library in Schaumburg, Illinois. She is the author of *Mind-Bending Mysteries and Thrillers for Teens: A Programming and Readers' Advisory Guide* (ALA Editions, 2014) and a coauthor of *A Year of Programs for Teens 2* (ALA Editions, 2011). Her first young adult mystery, *Taking the High Ground*, was published in 2013. Amy has been on the YALSA board of directors and enjoys offering presentations about library services or vintage cooking, her passion. She reviews for *Booklist* and *Crimespree Magazine*. She has a BS in criminology from the University of Illinois at Urbana-Champaign and an MLIS from Dominican University.

HEATHER BOOTH is committed to serving the dynamic needs and interests of young people in a community setting. She has been a teen services librarian in the Chicago suburbs since 2002, currently at the Thomas Ford Memorial Library in Western Springs, Illinois. She is the editor, with Karen Jensen, of *The Whole Library Handbook: Teen Services* (ALA Editions, 2014) and the author of *Serving Teens through Readers' Advisory* (ALA Editions, 2007). She also reviews, writes, and speaks on topics related to teen services and readers' advisory. She holds a BA from Kalamazoo College in southwestern Michigan and her library degree from the Graduate School of Library and Information Science at the University of Illinois at Urbana-Champaign.

© 2015 by the American Library Association

Extensive effort has gone into ensuring the reliability of the information in this book; however, the publisher makes no warranty, express or implied, with respect to the material contained herein.

ISBN: 978-0-8389-1334-5 (paper)

Library of Congress Cataloging-in-Publication Data

Alessio, Amy J.
  Club programs for teens : 100 activities for the entire year / by Amy Alessio and Heather Booth.
     pages cm
  Includes bibliographical references and index.
  ISBN 978-0-8389-1334-5 (print : alk. paper) 1. Young adults' libraries—Activity programs—United States. 2. Libraries and teenagers—United States. 3. Library clubs—United States. I. Booth, Heather, 1978- II. Title.
  Z718.5.A425 2015
  027.62'60973—dc23   2015004189

Cover design by Kimberly Thornton. Images © Shutterstock, Inc.
Text design by Alejandra Diaz in the Avenir, Alabama, and Charis SIL typefaces.

♾ This paper meets the requirements of ANSI/NISO Z39.48–1992 (Permanence of Paper).

Printed in the United States of America
19 18 17 16 15   5 4 3 2 1

DEDICATION

For my family, and all teens who help make
libraries into vibrant communities.
—AA—

For Paul, at last.
—HB—

CONTENTS

ACKNOWLEDGMENTS

It seems that teens inspire me during every shift at the Schaumburg Township District Library where it has been my privilege to work with them for the past nineteen years. It has also been my honor to see new, dynamic librarians join the field and ask me about my experiences. I marvel at how some of them do their work so much better than I've done mine. Heather Booth is one of those librarians. Without her creative energy, this book would not have come together. I am delighted that she joined me in writing about some of our favorite teen ideas and programs.

—AMY

Were it not for the teens that I have the pleasure to work with in the library, writing a book like this would have been impossible. I appreciate all of those teens who have let me get a glimpse into their lives and preferences at the library every day. I have enjoyed the generous professional guidance and friendship of Amy Alessio for a number of years, so getting a chance to contribute to this book with her was a joy. And finally I must thank my husband. When I asked what he thought of my working on another book, he never once reminded me that I was "taking a break," and didn't even roll his eyes when I told him I had already accepted the project. Thank you, Paul, for your constant encouragement and reassurance that this path is the right one.

—HEATHER

INTRODUCTION
Overview and Using This Book

Welcome to *Club Programs for Teens.* A good problem for libraries to have is a group of teens that grows increasingly bigger at each program until staff are unsure how to manage it. A huge group is still a challenge, and developing a teen club is a solution. What is a Teen Club? In many cases, it is a popular teen school or public library event that the teens want to revisit based on specific passions, such as writing, food, gaming, fashion, or green initiatives. The club could meet weekly, monthly, quarterly, or on a different recurring schedule agreeable to the staff and teens. Many times, a teen club grows from a successful teen program or develops from a strong teen interest in a particular topic, like anime and manga. Focusing on teen passion may help break up the unwieldy group into manageable sessions while encouraging teens to return and to focus on their interests at the library.

Why Should I Have Teen Clubs in My Library?

Teens have tight schedules these days and are used to regularly attending rehearsals, sports practices, and classes. Offering a consistently meeting club will help them remember to attend. Teens who come will get to know library staff and teens from other areas. Each person will learn more about others outside her immediate purview—and about how the library can serve her. This benefits the library in several ways. As more meetings on a theme continue, interest in that subject will grow, and library materials on that subject will be used more widely. Attending teens, as well as parents who bring them, will be exposed to new and more services and deepen their connection to the library. Teens will get to sample and explore new interests without investing time and money in expensive classes and lessons their family may not be able to afford, and parents will appreciate this aspect.

There are also benefits for library staff from offering a monthly club for teens. Staff will gain continuous feedback from teens—sometimes more than they would wish! That feedback will help staff plan more targeted and successful services for that age group. They will be able to have the regulars begin to lead programs and even apply to the library for future work positions.

A themed club makes planning programs easier, just as a summer reading theme can help inspire programs. If staff know a core group of teens will be coming each month, they can be confident that ideas with that theme will be favorably received. Offering a fashion or crafting program by itself may not garner teen attendance, depending on the date, time, or local competition for teen attention. But staff can have the club members engage in that activity at their prearranged time and know that some will be attending for sure.

Attending a library club contributes to healthy teen development. In addition to sharing positive experiences with the library and staff, a consistently attending teen will feel as if he belongs. Providing feedback and helping to run activities promote leadership skills and offer teens a feeling of ownership in the successful group. Getting to know teens from other schools expands their knowledge of their community and diversity.

A teen may have an interest in writing, but might not have time to add a creative writing course to a heavy school workload. Attending a library club allows her to write some poetry without worrying about a grade. Teens will feel comfortable trying new activities or library services within the comfort of club meetings or with library staff they have come to know well.

Tips for Building Clubs

Although library staff hope that teens will flock to the first, publicized meeting of a new group, it often takes some time for a club to grow. This section will provide ideas on starting a new group or growing a teen club organically from existing and popular teen services.

LET TEENS LEAD THE WAY

You know when teens are really interested in a topic. Registration lists will fill, many teens will come and want to stay beyond the formal program, materials on those topics will be checked out. Did way too many teens come to the Battle of the Bands night? Did the room fill for the *Divergent* party? Did the volunteering fair bring in more teens than there were jobs available? These are possible subjects for clubs. Before setting up a schedule of meetings in the next brochure, try some surveys with teens to discover when they can come and what topics intrigue them. Surveys may reach regular library users only, so be sure to try some methods to reach folks with the themed interest beyond regular library visitors. Post information about a new crafting for charity group with local church youth groups, craft stores, school volunteering clubs. Invite respondents to follow a link or fill out a paper survey. Host focus groups at different dates and times, or even at community areas such as a YMCA by offering pizza or snacks for teens who give up thirty to forty-five minutes providing feedback about a new library club. Poll library regulars about topics the schools do not cover, such as scrapbooking and photography, food clubs, and more. Or perhaps the schools offer those topics, but events or classes are hard to attend or so popular and crowded that teens would welcome another outlet for their interests at the library.

BUILD A BASE

To help kick things off, offer club meetings after other popular recurring events. For example, start the new Scrapbooking and Photography Club meetings right after the Teen Advisory Board meetings, especially if you know teens on the board may be interested. Offer incentives such as a couple of dollars off fines to teens who bring a friend to meetings. Have punch cards for meetings with prizes for frequent visitors.

Make meetings both productive and fun. Formal meetings with rules will turn off teens because of similarities to school. Basic rules, however, can be established to keep order without making participation rigid. Make some time to offer suggestions or go over club business at the beginning over snacks, followed by the themed activity, to satisfy both staff needs and teen interests.

Offer rewards to consistently attending members or to those who bring friends. This can be done by establishing a line of communication, such as e-mail or a Facebook, Yahoo!, Twitter, or Tumblr feed on the club. This gives staff a way to send reminders about the club and to keep teens tuning in to look for little bonuses, such as a fine-free coupon or a prize for the first few teens who respond to a request for feedback.

Be flexible. Welcoming newcomers each time keeps the groups going. Publish topics, speakers, or activities for some upcoming meetings to attract new folks. And be smart with these specialized promotions. A Green Teens Club is not going to appreciate lots of paper handouts. A Food Fan's attention will be caught by pictures of food. If attendance at a new club is slow to pick up, work on targeted promotion. Each club idea in this book will provide tips for promoting the club to teens.

Finally, try to build a constant connection with your new group. You can keep momentum going between meetings with displays, online links and lists, or tweets. Teen club members should see something new every couple of weeks at the library or on the websites that would appeal to them. Don't be afraid to try new formats. Most programs described in this book have online options or variations, and these can help inspire ideas. Are any teens visiting the library website or Facebook pages? Give them a reason to do so and keep trying. Invite teens to make their own video clips or tutorials on club topics to get attention. Libraries are always on the edge of new formats—show teens the truth of this.

KEEP IT REAL—FOR YOURSELF AND THEM

Planning for clubs can be easier than planning stand-alone programs. After a while, your base will be attending, and you just have to keep them interested with new session ideas. Teens who are coming will also have suggestions or may want to spend a couple of sessions on a popular topic. You should build on their suggestions. This will save you time and help build the group's popularity. Telling teens that their ideas could be implemented in the next fiscal year means nothing to them. Try to follow their suggestions as quickly as reasonably possible and let them know their suggestions are happening. This could be as simple as offering another session on a popular topic or activity, so they can work more on projects and try to do things differently.

No one has time to offer twelve clubs a year, and no teen has time to attend all those. If you simply don't have the time to offer one more thing, try some variations or online ideas or look hard at other offerings to see if programs can be combined or rescheduled.

Also, be sure to get help when you need it. We are definitely not experts on all the topics in this book. Amy Alessio, for example, hired a former teen art club member to run her computer animation classes as he had those skills. Teens like it when other teens teach. Is one teen really good at a craft? Solicit his help. Teens who teach can use the experience on résumés and applications, and if the library cannot pay them a fee, perhaps they would agree to be rewarded in other ways, such as with prizes. Some programs in this book require expert teachers, though not many. Self-Defense Basics in the Active Teens Club does require an expert, but Stop Motion Animation may not, with the help of tutorials. Teens often use the tutorials at home, so why not in a group where they can also help each other? In situations where your teens are eager to learn something but you lack a teen expert or funds to hire someone, do consider jumping in yourself as a facilitator for teens' own exploration instead of as an instructor. In doing so, you can demonstrate to teens that learning and trying new things are lifelong processes and that it's okay to try and fail and try again.

GIVE IT TIME

Groups generally require four to six months to catch on, which can be frustrating during the school year and as teens grow and move on to new sports and activities. But, it takes a while for new things to grow. Offering a club for a few months and then breaking off because of low attendance is not realistic. Staff time is gold, but give clubs a chance. If no one is coming, try a new time and date or even a quarterly schedule at first. Try out topics weekly or monthly in the summer to test the waters.

Try to build in flexibility for the future. The only constant in working with teens is change. A successful program this year may not be next year. Budgets need to be realistic but not rigid. Expect that staff will also change. Keep a file of ideas for future events or for programs that need to stop for a while or combine. Although administrative changes can be big surprises, often there are clues that new procedures are coming. For example, an administrator who has made it clear that she is not keen on craft programs may pull funding in favor of technology-themed events. Be prepared to morph those programs into something like Creative Computing to keep the teens and the administrator happy.

WHAT HAPPENS WHEN A CLUB DOES NOT WORK OR STOPS WORKING?

Teens are only teens for four to seven years if library services cover junior and senior high school ages. A group that is proactive and serious about art programs may age and fizzle out if no younger teens take up the interest. A group is no longer working when teens are not coming up with new ideas or when only a few come each month and just want to do a favorite social activity like playing board games and snacking. Although there is a place for those types of casual programs in the school or public library, they are not the focus of a club. Adult groups stall and change also—consider a book discussion group in which members who read each week and contribute ideas and discussion move away. What happens next?

Make sure the club is changing with the teens. If the same teens attend the Teen Advisory Board (TAB) for a few years, their interests and ability to work together are going to change. Do not stick to the same meeting procedures and rules. Even snack preferences and goals of the group are going to change. Certainly the goals and budgets of the library may change with new boards and personnel. Adaptability garners success and results in less stress for staff members.

Never permanently cancel a group that is no longer relevant. "I tried a teen group for a while, but no one came, so I canceled it" does not cut it with teen services. Think of how much technology has changed in the past five years. Have library programs and services kept in tune with teen trends as well? Teen services require constant feedback and adjustment.

All libraries have experienced failed teen programs that no one attends or in which things do not turn out well. Know when to change, end, and move on. Do not give up on programs, just reorganize them or take a break for a few months. Maybe the Teen Tasters session was so popular that a core group wants to do that at every meeting of the Food Fans Club. Break that group off into a separate club of themed tastings after the Food Fans Club meeting. Maybe lots of teens have grown out of the Teen Advisory Board and only a handful are attending who just want to talk about anime and manga. Help them form their own Anime and Manga Club, and get out the surveys to find out what younger teens want in terms of a Teen Advisory Board. After a break, start the board again with a new focus and possibly a new date and time. If you decide to take a break from a club for a few months, circulate a survey about times, dates, and interests among the teens who are coming to the library to see if a new time is needed or if the club needs a new focus. If a few teens are upset that the old club has been taken down, use their interests and efforts in planning a new one. Engage their help in volunteering in the meantime to keep them coming in to the library.

When it is time to restart an old club with a new focus or to establish a new club, spend time and effort on publicity—even more so than for other programs. Consider offering simple, easy applications for clubs even if all teens are accepted. Having teens list their interests and reasons for coming will solidify a vague interest in a poster they saw at the library into a commitment. Having teens fill out an application also weeds out those whose parent(s) may be forcing them to attend. If a public library is starting the program, staff should be sure that schools are well informed about it. Having expert speakers from school staff for clubs is a good way to keep that communication going—for example, you might pay a high school art teacher to run a creative teen event at a meeting.

There can be times when it seems no one is coming to teen programs. Offer a virtual club or chat times, or a virtual Teen Advisory Board, with rewards or occasional face-to-face meetings to keep feedback coming in until a new group of teens can be recruited for events.

Finally, sometimes clubs and programs are ended by administrators. Can you reach those teens online or through events that meet less often? Do topics need adjustment to better tie in with current library themes? Dealing with this reality can be painful, but a new, exciting program may come from it, so do not let it discourage you.

How to Use This Book

In each of the themed chapters in this book, we present a club for teens with at least seven ideas for meetings, with most programs offering suggestions for variations and online aspects. It is expected that some of the topics from other clubs may cross over or that clubs might not meet for all twelve months of the year. Libraries that do not have the staff or space to offer a monthly club on some of these themes can try out a described meeting as a stand-alone program or select programs across themes to accommodate other themes, such as state summer reading initiatives.

The Read-a-Latte Books and Media discussion group is presented differently than the other clubs. Ideas for twelve themes, such as Out of This World (science fiction) or Teens Get Real with Reading (nonfiction), are described, rather than broken out into separate sessions. The Read-a-Latte Books and Media Club will use the same format for each meeting with little in the way of themed props other than snacks or simple decorations. Libraries that are new to club programming may well be accustomed to, or at least familiar with, book clubs and can easily use the Read-a-Latte format to discover which topics and interests held by book club teens might be spun off into new clubs.

Libraries with long-standing Teen Advisory Boards or other popular clubs will find further ideas in the chapter titled More Ideas for Established Clubs. Ideas for other groups in that chapter pull from themes throughout this book to offer suggestions for advisory boards, writing clubs, creative or crafty groups, teens who meet to discuss volunteering and community service projects, money management clubs, technology-themed groups, drama clubs, or a monthly club of teens dedicated to making movies.

Each club description begins with an introductory page offering some ideas for Power Promotion and listing any Crossover Programs. Crossovers are sessions described for one club that will appeal to at least one other club as well. For example, Ancient Fashions, a session from the Fashionista Teens Club in which teens learn about ancient

Greek and Roman fashions and make togas and laurel wreaths, should also appeal to members of the Traveling Teens Club. A session on Rain Barrel Decoration for the Green Teens Club could also be a session for the Crafting for Charity Club. The two clubs could meet together for that topic, or the same idea could be used twice, saving staff preparation time.

Details for each club program are provided under the following headings.

CROSSOVER

If the meeting topic could also be used for a different club, that information is provided here as well as on the introductory page.

SHOPPING LIST

Many ideas presented in this book require no purchases, but audiovisual equipment may be needed, such as a laptop and projector.

MAKE IT HAPPEN

This part presents activities for each club meeting. Some of the sessions will require teens to view tutorials, and you will want to view them first. Information may change online.

It is expected that promotion of events takes place three to six months prior in public libraries especially, but some of the activities include extra suggestions to help advertise the events.

VARIATIONS

Most club session ideas are followed by variations, both physical and virtual, for different library situations, such as school library settings.

ONLINE

Many club session ideas also contain ways to continue the topic online after the meeting.

RESOURCES

Some club sessions have resources listed here, but many include links to tutorials or information in the Make It Happen section. With many nonfiction topics, you are always encouraged to pull some general books, magazines, or media on those topics for interested teens, but no list of titles is required for these programs.

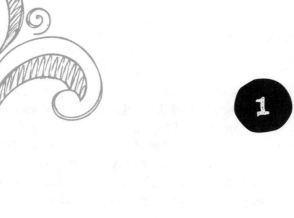

Read-a-Latte Books and Media Club
A Gateway Club

This club may inspire more clubs! That is, each program may produce passionate teens who want to continue the activities or topic. Many of the topics will naturally lend themselves to crossover programming with other clubs. Teens who want to discuss more nonfiction books may continue the discussion online or at the next meeting, if they prefer that genre to others. Being flexible will help teens in this group find their footing.

Read-a-Latte sessions will each feature a genre reflected in either books or movies. Teens can bring a favorite title in that genre, and the group leader can booktalk other titles they may enjoy. Teens may also view a movie or recorded television program in that genre as part of the program. Rather than focus on one title and require teens to each read their own copy, this casual group introduces book and movie lovers to more of what they enjoy.

SHOPPING LIST

- Refreshments (Tips for refreshments for particular themes are noted in the following Make It Happen section.)

MAKE IT HAPPEN

- At the first meeting, invite interested teens to fill out an easy questionnaire about their favorite titles and genres.
- Or, just discuss favorite books or movies and then have refreshments and watch a popular movie.

- Teens may want to choose the genre for the next meeting. Invite them to check the library social media site to find suggested titles in that genre and to leave comments and ideas.
- At other themed nights, provide a cart of books and media or a list of items that match the next session's theme.
- Each month should have themed activities. A few are suggested here, but teens may have more—and better—ideas!

Award-Winning Readers: This session could feature local, national, or library-level awards. Gold coins or blue ribbon decorations and a decorated voting box may add to the awards theme.

- Teens' Choice Award: Invite teens to develop their own award and mark the book spines of teen favorites to start. Other teen library patrons could then vote for their favorites among those titles in person or online.
- General Award Booktalking: Before the meeting, pull some titles that have received a state or other award for teen literature. Invite teens to describe any books from the selection that they may have read and be prepared to describe the rest in a formal booktalk or a more casual presentation. Invite teens to discuss what they would like to read and why. Discuss whether award-winning titles are attractive or a turnoff.
- Crossover: The Newsworthy Teens Club can write about the awards and winners and losers or create a sports bracket–style "book-off" system to guess the winners of next year's major book awards.

Romantic Readers: This theme would be fun for Valentine's Day, but the books do not have to have a happy ending. The theme could be changed a bit to Un-Romantic Readers, especially if many boys have been attending the club. Use black paper goods for serving snacks and scatter broken paper hearts on the table.

- Tragically Romantic: Pull some books with sad romantic endings, such as *The Fault in Our Stars* by John Green. Ask teens how they feel about the way *Romeo and Juliet* ends. Compare it to some teen books and ask why reading those types of books is appealing.
- What Makes a Good Romance? Pull titles from the Romance Writers of America (RWA) Young Adult Romance award category and ask teens which ones they have read. Discuss why those titles won awards or nominations and explore what teens feel a good romantic relationship should include (in both fiction and real life).
- Crossover: Fashionista Teens can adapt the Trashion Show, Retro Fashions, or Ancient Fashions programs to create costumes for their favorite romantic characters.

Fantastic Readers: Refreshments can range from elf cakes to butterbeer for this month. Tie-ins to upcoming movies can be a natural fit for this as well, or host a viewing of *The Lord of the Rings*, *The Avengers*, *Harry Potter*, or other popular fantasy adventures.

- Fantastic Weapons: Invite teens to discuss the coolest weapon they have read about in a fantasy book and what type they would like to have. Provide duct tape and large cardboard pieces for a post-discussion sword-making activity.

- Creative Creatures: Teens can discuss favorite creatures, such as why dragons may not make good pets. After the discussion, invite them to draw the fantasy creature they most remember or would most like to have.
- Crossover: For the Green Teens Club's Reuse–Remake–Renew program, create scenery or significant props (amulets, shields) from materials at hand.

Out of This World: Space and stars are a natural decoration theme for this meeting.
- Steampunk Ships: Pull a selection of steampunk books for teens and discuss why Victorian elements or fantastic traveling ships are so important to that genre. Ask teens what period in time they would like to travel to. What kind of machine would they use for travel or transportation? Consider offering a steampunk gear–themed craft as an additional activity.
- Back to the Future: Which elements of classic science fiction books have come true? Read quotes or descriptions from *1984, 2001: A Space Odyssey,* or Verne's *Journey to the Center of the Earth* and ask teens how those imagined technologies became reality in the modern day. What current science fiction authors do teens enjoy? What predictions have they read in science fiction that they believe may come true?
- Crossovers: Use the Green Teens Club's Reuse–Remake–Renew program to create steampunk-inspired objects. At the Spin-Off Challenge program for the Scientific Teens Club, spin technologies in the books into real life.

Teens Get Real with Reading: Nonfiction fans may want their own themed book club with a different subject featured each month. Others may want to know about some good ones at one of the Read-a-Latte Club meetings.
- YALSA Alex and Nonfiction Awards: The YALSA Alex Awards honor titles published for adults that are also excellent reading for teens. Many are nonfiction, and of course, the Excellence in Nonfiction Awards are another place to find titles to feature at the meeting. After describing some of those noted titles, ask teens which books might appeal to them and why.
- Beyond Biographies: What subject do teens in the club want to learn more about but don't have time? Help them find the section on those books in the library, whether it's cookbooks, history, hobbies, or occult books, and invite them to talk about those subjects at the meeting before checking out titles to take home.
- Crossovers: The Newsworthy Teens Club can use the reporting strategies in their programs to report on the stories from these books. If the nonfiction reading spurs teens to undertake social justice work, the Crafting for Charity Club can use the crafts described to make a difference.

Author Event: Invite a local author to host a Read-a-Latte Club meeting, or arrange a Skype visit with an author chosen by the teens. Give teens a copy of this author's most recent book ahead of time so they may be prepared with questions.
- Crossovers: Newsworthy Teens can take this opportunity to report on the exciting event. Entertaining Teens can share their writing with the author (if he or she consents). Use the Taking the Fear Out of Public Speaking program to prepare teens ahead of time so no one is too starstruck and tongue-tied.

Book to Movie Club: Many popular teen books are being made into movies. Consider showing the movie before, during, or after the monthly meeting and asking teens to compare the two versions.

- Clips: Showing clips of pivotal scenes or interviews with actors (from the extra features on the DVD) is another fun way to compare the movie to the book.
- Movie Planning: After viewing a movie, ask teens what book should be made into a movie and who should be in it. Or, ask them to recast and change a current movie to their liking.
- Crossovers: The Traveling Teens' Armchair Traveler Movie Nights are a great fit for this club. Newsworthy Teens can use the discussion as the jumping-off point for a dueling critics movie review feature on the library blog or other teen writing venue.

Mad about Music and Movies: The movie theme may be popular enough to develop into a quarterly or monthly club of its own. For example, the first movie in a planned trilogy could be shown before the second one hits the theaters. Or activities could be planned to go with an upcoming movie event.

- Act Out Song Titles: Club members may be interested in discussing soundtracks for authors or movies. Many authors list what music should go with their books, and some research ahead of time could lead to a mini trivia game on this subject. Invite teens to match songs to movies or books in discussion.
- And the Winner Is: Music and movies have televised awards. Invite teens to discuss why books do not get similar treatment and how that would be handled if they did. What categories would members like to see, and what books would they nominate in those categories?
- Crossovers: Active Teens can get involved in making workout playlists. Entertaining Teens will have lots to discuss as they critique acting styles, staging, costuming, music choices, and the like.

Mind-Bending Mysteries: In her book *Mind-Bending Mysteries and Thrillers for Teens*, Amy Alessio outlined a year of activities for a Mystery Club. A few ideas to get started are listed here.

- Types of Mysteries: Discuss the differences between thrillers, romantic suspense, nonfiction true crime, and paranormal mysteries and invite teens to talk about which elements they like best. Be prepared with examples.
- Mystery Madness: Set up a mini crime scene by scattering items such as a shoe, a phone, crumpled paper, and the like at the front of the room and invite teens to discuss what happened and why they think so. This could also be done online with photographs.
- Crossovers: Newsworthy Teens can use the mini crime scene as the impetus for fictional news stories in conjunction with the Deadline! program. For Scientific Teens, the Forensic Fun program is an ideal pairing for mystery fans.

Serious about Series: Both teens and adults love series, and often they are ignored by awards and suggested lists of books. At this themed meeting invite teens to talk about favorite series. Ask how many books they like to see in a series before it no longer appeals to them.

- Series Standouts: Have teens list favorites. Put together a list of the most popular ones by compiling some circulation statistics (or by looking at what is not on the shelves) and see how they compare.
- Series, Sequels, and Trilogies: Provide examples of each and ask teens if stories should be continued if the author dies or in new variations, such as the Jane Austen variations in adult books. Should more people be writing Sherlock Holmes books? Bring variations to compare and ask teens what series they would like to see in new forms.
- Crossover: Because of the die-hard nature of so many series fans, these teens make ideal interview candidates for aspiring journalists or subjects for the Interview Skills program of the Newsworthy Teens Club.

Anime and Manga Readers and Viewers: Often huge readers, fans of these genres may want their own club, but they definitely deserve attention in any reading program or promotion.
- Super Readers: Younger teens may want to talk about comics or superhero series. Invite a comic book store owner or devoted teen reader to lead the discussion on best characters, the history of those characters, and changes. Invite teens to invent their own super persona and describe their costumes and powers.
- Animania: Highlight favorite classic manga and anime series and discuss other series that are read-alikes. Ask teens if fans of manga romance would enjoy non-illustrated books on those topics and if so, which ones. Consider serving Pocky at this meeting.
- Crossover: The Technology Makers' Stop Motion Animation and Introduction to Computer Animation programs are natural fits for anime fans to explore. Manga fans may enjoy further exploring their favorite format in comparison with other illustration styles in the Newsworthy Teens' Cartoon Capers program.

Favorite Children's Titles: Who doesn't like to revisit favorite books? This month's theme helps teens remember why they liked children's books.
- Teen Storytime: Bring club members to the youth area to rediscover favorite authors and books. Each teen can take a picture book back to the meeting to pass or read and share.
- Rerun Readers: Ask teens to write down the titles of five books they owned or read several times in grade school and compare lists. Ask them why they remember those titles rather than others.
- Crossover: After reminiscing about their favorite childhood books, Active Teens Club members can get up and moving in the Active Inner Child program by remembering their favorite playground games.

POWER PROMOTION

- Post the next session's theme in a prominent location with a matching book and movie list and a display of those items where possible.
- Also have a cart with materials for the next session at each meeting to help teens think ahead.
- Putting bookmarks with a list of themes and dates in matching books will attract attention. These could also be put in reserves waiting to be picked up to catch readers who may not know about library programs.

Active Teens

Fitness and health are important topics for teens, and this club makes it fun. By looking at new tools and different ways to move, teens will challenge themselves and others to find ways to enjoy getting and staying healthy.

POWER PROMOTION

- Before this club begins, consider handing out granola bars with information about the first meeting wrapped around the wrappers.
- Set up a "relaxation station"—a table or corner in the teen area with information about the Active Teens Club, basic stretching, yoga, smoothie recipes, and other materials designed to help teens de-stress.
- Another approach is to play soothing music for a few minutes at the same time each evening for a week and encourage teens to join you for a few stretches. They may laugh, but if they do it, the stretches will help those bodies that are cramped at school and in front of homework all day and night.

CROSSOVER PROGRAMS

- Just Juggling—Entertaining Teens
- Geocaching—Scientific Teens
- Travel Vision Board—Traveling Teens

➡ Fitness Challenge

Inspire teens to increase the number of steps they take per day with a Fitness Challenge! The recommended number of steps is 15,000 per day for teen boys and 12,000 per day for teen girls. At the previous meeting, teens can sign up, get a pedometer, and agree to follow the challenge for at least one week before returning the pedometer. Teens with cell phones may choose to install apps for tracking steps instead, if they are allowed to keep their phone with them at all times during the day.

SHOPPING LIST

- Inexpensive pedometers for teens who register for the challenge
- Prizes for teens who complete the challenge (gift certificates to frozen yogurt shops, fine-off coupons, and the like)

MAKE IT HAPPEN

- Register teens for the challenge and give each a pedometer.
- Have teens record their steps each day for at least a week.
- Award a prize to girls who reach 12,000 steps and to boys who reach 15,000 by the end of the challenge. An alternate way to award prizes is by percentage increase—for example, teens who increase their number of steps by 30 percent receive a prize.
- Have teens send final totals to you in e-mail for privacy.

VARIATIONS

- Club Challenge: Teens can choose a goal for the group at the beginning of the week and if the group reaches the steps goal together, they all get a prize. For example, a group of teens would have to reach 144,000 steps in a week.
- Activity Time Challenge: This program could be done without pedometers by asking teens to record the amount of time spent doing active things with a goal of sixty minutes per day.

ONLINE

- Place a graph on the teen site showing their progress toward the goal each day based on recorded entries.
- Use e-mail to send daily tips on how to increase steps or post on the library teen Facebook page or Twitter stream.

RESOURCES

Map Pedometer: www.mappedometer.com
Presidential Youth Fitness Program Downloadable Log Sheets: www.presidentschallenge.org/tools-resources/forms.shtml

◧ Self-Defense Basics

All teens should learn basic self-defense. Between working night hours, traveling home after dark from activities, and coping with the escalating rate of dating violence, teens clearly need to know how to protect themselves. This topic is best addressed by police personnel or martial arts instructors, but library staff can supplement that information.

MAKE IT HAPPEN

- At least one month prior to the club session on self-defense, fill out the form on the website for *Just Yell Fire*, a self-defense movie for teen girls ages 12 to 19, and show the movie at the club meeting (www.justyellfire.com/movie .php?video = Just_Yell_Fire_Movie). The website also has a section with additional materials for educators.
- Contact your local police department and a local martial arts training academy and ask if someone will talk to the teens about self-defense and perhaps demonstrate techniques. Many studios will do this for little or no cost if they can advertise their business to prospective martial arts students. They may require waivers to be signed by parents before teaching self-defense moves to teens during the meeting.
- Invite teens to share situations that make them feel unsafe and discuss how to avoid those. Give club members fictional scenarios if they are uncomfortable sharing. For example, a teen girl's boyfriend shoves her into the wall. What should she do next? A teen boy's girlfriend slaps him or twists his arm and pretends she is joking. What happens then? Or a teen is at a dance when her date gets aggressive. How can that be avoided?
- Make a bookmark with the phone numbers for local rape crisis centers, domestic violence hotlines, and other local organizations that help teen victims. These links should also be available online.

ONLINE

- Links abound for self-defense websites, but they can contradict each other. Getting live training is best. If a speaker is available for this session, ask if parts of the session may be filmed for the teen website.

→ Library Garden

Gardening is active work, and the Active Teens can work with the Green Teens in a library or community garden. Produce could go to a local food pantry.

CROSSOVER

- Green Teens

SHOPPING LIST

- Basic gardening supplies (fertilizer [organic if possible], rake, watering can, wooden stakes and string, trowel, shovel)
- Containers for planting herbs or small tomato plants if a garden space is not available (optional)
- Seeds (pepper, carrot, and tomato seeds to begin or other crops based on local climate)

MAKE IT HAPPEN

- Consult with staff who garden, library administration, and a local garden club if available to determine the parameters of the garden and rules for operation. For example, the garden club may choose to work with the teens to set up a care schedule and to deal with pest issues. Library maintenance may also wish to be consulted about how the project will run and how tools will be stored.
- In the spring, have teens turn over the dirt in the designated area. A small square is a great way to test out the project the first year. If no space is available, consider letting teens maintain plants in a sunny area of the library or on the roof.
- Work with teens to assign chores and dates for garden care, such as weeding and watering.
- Plant seeds at appropriate times. To track progress, teens can take photos at meetings and when they care for the plants. The number of vegetables grown is another good record to keep. When food is harvested, it should be washed and donated locally.
- Publicize the location in library brochures and on signs so other patrons will know this is a library project and, it is hoped, will respect the space.

VARIATIONS

- Seed Swap: Invite patrons to bring in packets of seeds they don't need and swap them for others. A decorated box in a makerspace is all that is needed for the swap.
- Indoor Library Makerspace with Plants: Having plants in an indoor makerspace keeps the project going year-round. Lighting may not be a reasonable cost at first, so herbs or small vegetable boxes could be maintained in sunny spots.

ONLINE

- Garden Blog: A blog charting the garden's progress can be maintained by the teens (with help from staff if necessary) throughout the warm season to keep momentum going on the project.

RESOURCES

Bonnie Plants Site Library (information on indoor, community, and herb gardens and more):
http://bonnieplants.com/library/how-to-grow-herbs-indoors
National Gardening Association: www.garden.org

⮕ Decades of Dance Moves

Teens can get active by dancing and can learn some retro moves at this interactive event. Library staff may have moves from their past to bring out, but no doubt instructional DVDs still exist in the library collection for the Electric Slide and other dances. Online tutorials are another option.

CROSSOVER

- Entertaining Teens

SHOPPING LIST

- Provide cups and water. Teens should be advised ahead of time to wear comfortable, workout-type clothing.

MAKE IT HAPPEN

Clear a space to practice some dance moves with the teens. Allow for projection from a computer or DVD player so they can follow along.

- 1940s: Help teens learn some basic Swing and Lindy Hop moves with this easy-to-follow tutorial: http://tag.wonderhowto.com/1940s-swing-dance.
- 1950s: Show a clip from Grease illustrating the Hand Jive. The web page "50s Dance Moves" (http://dance.lovetoknow.com/dance-instruction/50s-dance-moves) also breaks down instructions for the Cha-Cha and the Stroll.
- 1960s: Get out Chubby Checker music and encourage teens to Twist, like they did last summer . . . .
- 1960s: Help teens learn to do the Mashed Potato, Watusi, and more with this site: www.the60sofficialsite.com/Dance_Crazes_of_the_60s.html.
- 1970s: Introduce the disco era with a dance everyone knows—YMCA—then move on to other funky disco moves like the Bus Stop and the Hustle: http://lite987.com/five-iconic-dances-of-the-70s-videos.
- 1980s: The Moonwalk, the Electric Slide, the Sprinkler, and more are right here for teens to learn: www.buzzfeed.com/breakoutband/90s-music-video-dance-moves-32ip.

VARIATIONS

- Zumba: Invite a local zumba instructor (or break out the library DVDs again) to teach teens some basic moves for a fun workout.

→ Smoothie Station

Smoothies are an easy and fun way to try new fruits and veggies, are a healthy option for snacking and breakfasts, and are an appealing option for active, health-conscious teens. In this program, you'll provide teens with a variety of smoothie ingredients and let them create and name their masterpieces.

CROSSOVER

- Food Fans

SHOPPING LIST

- Cups
- Plastic table covers
- Blender(s)
- Dish soap
- Measuring cups and spoons

Smoothie Ingredients (a variety from each category)

MAIN FLAVORS
- Fresh or frozen fruits
- Fresh or frozen vegetables
- Oats or other edible raw grains

PROTEINS
- Nuts or nut butters
- Silken tofu
- Yogurt

LIQUIDS
- Fruit juice
- Coconut milk
- Milk, almond milk, soy milk
- Ice

ADD-INS
- Honey or other sweeteners
- Spices and herbs like cinnamon or mint

MAKE IT HAPPEN

- Prepare the space—cover the tables and set out the blenders, ingredients, and measuring tools.
- Invite teens to combine ingredients to create their favorite flavor blends, then pour them out into cups. Encourage teens to name their flavor mashups and offer them for others to sample.

ONLINE

- Share pictures and recipes for the favorite creations.

RESOURCES

Pinterest.com is a great place to find classic and trendy smoothie combinations.

➡ Chill-Out Yoga

The ancient practice of yoga has gotten pretty flashy of late. But at its core, it's a gentle, meditative practice that honors the body of the participant in whatever shape it takes. Yoga is a great complement to active teen lives as it encourages a thoughtfulness about the mind-body connection and moves at the participant's own pace.

SHOPPING LIST

- Teens should wear comfortable clothes and bring a large towel or mat.
- If you plan to show yoga video clips, a computer or DVD player and projector and screen will be needed.

MAKE IT HAPPEN

- Contact local yoga studios or instructors and ask if anyone would be willing to either lead your teens through a session of yoga or just talk about the practice of yoga.
- Play some gentle, soothing music or nature sounds to set the mood as teens enter the room. Dim the lighting if possible.
- Have teens spread out around the room and find a comfortable seated position on their towel or mat.
- Talk about some of the basic safety principles of yoga. Nothing should be painful, and teens need to stop if any movement becomes so. Alignment is important to protect joints—remind teens to never hyperextend and to focus on keeping the spine aligned correctly throughout the poses. If you are not a trained yoga instructor, you should not attempt to correct the alignment of the kids in your group. Just verbally point out to them items that they can check themselves. The breath is important—remind teens to take gentle, full breaths throughout. For a tutorial on yogic breathing, see www.mindbodygreen.com/ 0-6751/Mastering-the-Full-Yogic-Breath.html.

- Encourage teens to move with you—or with a video—through some basic poses. Common "flows" like the Sun Salutation are sets of yoga poses that move naturally from one to the next.
- End the session by having teens lie comfortably on their backs and focus on breathing before easing out of the yoga session.

VARIATIONS

- There are so many ways to practice yoga—if your teens would prefer a more energetic practice, or one that is intended to complement running, or one that is specific to stress reduction, there are classes, instructors, and videos for that!

RESOURCES

20-Minute Yoga Class for Beginners: www.mindbodygreen.com/0-6751/Mastering-the-Full -Yogic-Breath.html

Top 10 Beginner Yoga Poses: www.youtube.com/watch?v=2D5Zq4wNK_s

◧ Active Inner Child

If we all moved as joyfully and frequently as little kids do, we'd all be in great shape. This program encourages teens to get in touch with their inner child as they have fun being active with playground games from their youth.

CROSSOVER

- Favorite Children's Titles—Read-a-Latte Books and Media Club

SHOPPING LIST

- Playground balls (optional)

MAKE IT HAPPEN

This program requires a large space free of obstructions. Outside is ideal, but a gymnasium is great and a large meeting room will do as well.

Red Rover: For this game, have teens form two groups. Each team will join hands in a line on opposite sides of a field of play. Team A starts by chanting, "Red rover, red rover, let [name] come over." That person leaves team A to run toward team B. If that person can break through the clasped hands, he gets to bring one person from team B back to team A. If not, that person joins team B. Remind teens to clasp hands without entwining fingers and be playfully competitive but cautious—they're all a lot faster and stronger than they were as 8-year-olds!

Tag: Who could forget Tag? One person is "It" and the others run away. Once tagged, the next person becomes It. Variations include Statue Tag (each tagged person freezes—the last one unfrozen is the winner), Zombie Tag (each tagged person also becomes It—the last one untagged is the winner), or Blob Tag (each tagged person holds hands with "It" until the blob has absorbed all the players).

Leapfrog: Teens form a line, crouching down on hands and knees or bending over while bracing hands on thighs. The last person in line jumps over those in front by placing her hands on the back of the person in front for extra boost. She becomes the first person in line, and then the now last person begins jumping.

Sharks and Minnows: One person is the shark and stands in the middle of the field of play. The others are minnows and gather at one side of the field. The minnows chant "Sharky, sharky, may we pass?" and the shark replies, "Only if you . . ." and then names a characteristic: have brown hair, are wearing red shoes, go to X school, and so forth. Those people then race to the opposite end of the field. If the shark tags any minnows, they become seaweed and have to stay where they were tagged until all minnows have been caught.

Duck, Duck, Goose: Players sit in a circle. A goose is chosen who walks the perimeter of the circle tapping the heads of the other players, saying "Duck, duck, duck" for each, until saying "Goose!" for one. The person tagged as the goose gets up from the circle and chases the tagger around the circle. If the goose can catch the tagger, he can reclaim his spot, and the tagger runs another round. If the tagger makes it all the way around the circle into the goose's spot, the goose becomes the new tagger.

VARIATIONS

- Any number of playground games would work for this program—Kickball, Dodgeball, Four Square, and so on.

RESOURCES

Go Out and Play! Favorite Outdoor Games from Kaboom! Candlewick Press, 2012.
   List of Traditional Children's Games: http://en.wikipedia.org/wiki/List_of_traditional
   _children%27s_games
Strother, Scott. *The Adventurous Book of Outdoor Games: Classic Fun for Daring Boys and Girls.*
   Sourcebooks, 2008.

Crafting for Charity

Teens today like to volunteer and help others. This club combines creativity with good works as teens make things or raise money to help those in need. Groups in need of donations of everything from pet blankets to scarves, gloves, or baby hats are likely present in the library community, but there are national organizations and drives also. Letting teens have input about who will get helped from the projects adds value. To inspire and reward teens, consider taking them on a tour to the hospital or shelter where donations are being used.

POWER PROMOTION

- Like other craft programs, photos and displays of made objects help promote this program. The website should list organizations helped and supplies or objects needed.
- Having a contest to obtain fifty baby hats during Teen Read Week will invite others in the community to help and spotlight the good work of this group.

CROSSOVER PROGRAMS

- Quilled Cards—Scrapbooking and Photography
- Simple Scarves—Fashionista Teens
- Rain Barrel Decoration—Green Teens
- Forcing Potted Bulbs—Green Teens
- Reuse–Remake–Renew—Green Teens

◾ Not So Squared

Great for beginners, this program teaches basic knitting or crocheting and helps beginners fashion squares for charities that assemble blankets. Some teens may do so well that they could keep working on the square until it is actually a scarf. If there is a lot of interest in making squares, this program is a good leadoff for the Warm-Up Challenge, the program featured next.

SHOPPING LIST

- These items may be donated to the library for this project. Not much yarn is needed to make squares.
- Worsted weight yarn (be aware that some charities request easy-wash acrylic yarns for squares)
- Size 8 or 9 straight knitting needles *or* size I-9 crochet hook
- Tape measures
- Scissors

MAKE IT HAPPEN

- Prepare copies of instructions for casting on and knitting the basic garter stitch or for doing the basic crochet double stitch. Project tutorials during the session for teens to reference.
- Teens will need to cast on at least thirty to thirty-five stitches to make 7-inch squares (some charities may request larger squares).
- If teens are familiar with knitting or crocheting, invite them to make a different pattern on their squares.
- Teens should be able to knit at least a few rows during the meeting and can bring back finished projects in the future or for help binding them off.
- When several squares have been gathered, have teens help pack them up and label for mailing with a note signed by all crafters.

VARIATIONS

- Structure this as a self-directed program coordinated by your club teens by providing instructions and supplies in the teen area. Interested teens may be encouraged to join the club for future events!
- If your teens are unfamiliar with knitting and crocheting techniques, invite your library's knitting club to help work with the teens in a cross-generational event.

ONLINE

- Links to organizations collecting squares and to tutorials can be posted on the library website with an appeal for squares. Updates on how many have been turned in and pictures can add momentum.
- Run online contests of total knitted versus crocheted squares that have been donated.

Springfield Stitches for a Cause (collects squares that are 12 by 12 inches):
www.facebook.com/pages/Springfield-Stitches-for-a-Cause/151415681555868

Warm Up America (this site has basic knitting and crocheting patterns for squares):
www.warmupamerica.org

⊡ Warm-Up Challenge

Building on the knitted square sessions, this session draws the programs together to collect blankets. Some teens can assemble squares into blankets while others pack or prepare finished blankets for shipping or delivery.

SHOPPING LIST

- Yarn for sewing squares together
- Large yarn needles
- Boxes for shipping
- Shipping labels
- Markers

MAKE IT HAPPEN

- Teens comfortable with this step can lay out blanket squares and whipstitch them together into blankets.
- The rest of the group can fold and pack blankets for shipping or donating.

VARIATIONS

- Partner with another library to have a blanket-drive competition and post resulting totals.
- Post how many blankets were collected in previous years and set a higher goal for this year with updates.

ONLINE

- On the library teen site, post the number of blankets assembled and donated with photos of the blankets and the donation sites if possible.

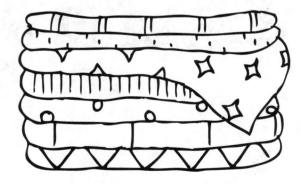

⬛ Denim Dog Toys

Teens use discarded jeans to create chew toys that can be donated to pet rescue organizations, the Humane Society, or a local Read to the Dogs program.

CROSSOVER

- Green Teens

SHOPPING LIST

- Jeans (donated or purchased at a thrift shop)
- Scissors
- Plastic squeakers (optional; found at craft stores)

MAKE IT HAPPEN

Instruct teens on how to make the toys.
- Cut the jeans into strips. Remove metal pieces like zippers and rivets.
- Braid, knot, or twist the strips into different shapes. Be sure that all knots are tight so the toy provides tougher chewing for the dog.
- For squeaky toys, cut the legs off a pair of jeans and place a squeaker into each tube created. Make a knot on either side of the squeaker, and continue knotting down the leg, inserting a squeaker into every other pocket. Cut the jeans so that each piece has a squeaker in the center. (Imagine how a piece of hard candy is wrapped: the jeans are the wrapper, and the squeaker is the candy.)

▣ Comfort Packs for the Homeless

This activity may take a few sessions, as teens will need to collect items to include. Consider posting a request in the library for the small items in the shopping list and inviting community members to contribute donations. A comfort pack includes small niceties, compactly packaged, that can be donated to a local homeless shelter.

SHOPPING LIST

- Quart-size ziplock bags
- Labels
- Markers

A variety of comfort items such as:

- Travel-size toothpaste
- Travel-size shampoo and conditioner
- Travel-size hand lotion
- Lip balm
- Tissues
- Single-use packs of common OTC medications like pain relievers or cold medicine
- Hand warmers
- Candy
- Snacks (nuts, granola bars, and the like)
- Single-serving packs of instant coffee or hot chocolate
- Tea bags
- Razors
- Sanitary supplies
- Socks

MAKE IT HAPPEN

- Encourage teens to gather supplies. This may take several weeks if they are relying on donations.
- Have teens choose a target charity and find out if it has any requirements or restrictions for receiving donations like this.
- Set up the room assembly line–style.
- Have teens either fill a bag or pass the bag down the line for filling.
- Finish by inviting teens to add a handwritten label to each bag with words of care and kindness.

VARIATIONS

- Comfort packs like this could also be distributed to communities after natural disasters or to domestic violence shelters.

RESOURCES

Blessing Backpack Checklist: http://homesweetroad.com/wp-content/uploads/2013/11/ Blessing-Backpack-Printable.pdf

⮕ Color a Smile

Color a Smile is an organization that provides coloring sheets and then collects them to distribute to people who need a pick-me-up: military service members, senior citizens in independent living facilities, and nursing home residents. It's as simple as it sounds: color a picture, make someone smile. This is a simple activity that would be a nice way to show off your Crafting for Charity Club at an open house, a library-wide event like the summer reading kickoff, or an anniversary or grand opening. This is also a handy activity to have at the ready if other programs or meetings run short and you're looking for something to fill time. It's also nice as a self-directed activity in the teen space.

CROSSOVER

- Favorite Children's Titles—Read-a-Latte Books and Media Club (use this activity to set the mood before discussing childhood favorites)
- Active Inner Child—Active Teens (provide these coloring sheets as a wind-down activity)

SHOPPING LIST

- Printouts of the Color a Smile pages: http://colorasmile.org/volunteer (be sure to provide some pictures and some blank pages)
- Crayons, markers, and the like

MAKE IT HAPPEN

- Print out the Color a Smile sheets.
- Provide space for relaxing and coloring.
- Play some music to lighten the mood.
- Have some fun!

VARIATIONS

- You need not work directly with this organization. Teens can color or draw and deliver pictures directly to nursing homes or assisted living facilities, children's hospitals, or homeless shelters in your community.
- This makes a good introduction and welcome for younger kids or tweens who may be interested in joining a Crafting for Charity group later on.

RESOURCES

Color a Smile: http://colorasmile.org

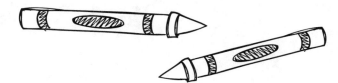

Pillowcases for Teens

Club members sew or decorate colorful pillowcases with personality to give to teens in the foster care system or in homeless shelters. As teens enter a difficult situation or are moved from place to place, having small, useful items that are clearly identifiable as their own can be a real comfort. This project can scale up or down depending on the skill level of your group. At its simplest, the session involves embellishing plain white pillowcases using permanent markers or paint pens. If your library has access to sewing machines, collect colorful, fun fabric and use this as a basic sewing project. Consider adding personal items that everyone needs, such as candy, lip balm, deodorant, a card, lotion, a toothbrush, shampoo, and the like, to the pillowcase.

SHOPPING LIST

Embellished Pillowcases
- Pillowcases (donated or purchased at thrift shops)
- Sharpies or paint markers
- Ribbons, buttons, beads, and other embellishments
- Fabric glue *or* needle and thread
- Iron and ironing board

Sewn Pillowcases
- Fabric
- Scissors
- Sewing machines
- Thread

MAKE IT HAPPEN

Embellished Pillowcases
- Give each teen a pillowcase and talk about the need for personal items that are easily identifiable. Discuss the issues of teen homelessness and the challenges faced by teens in foster care.
- Encourage teens to use the markers or paint pens to decorate the pillowcases with bright, cheerful, empowering but nonjudgmental imagery and words. (Phrases like "sweet dreams" or "good night" are appropriate for anyone, whereas "God bless you" or similarly religious phrases may not be well received by some.) If teens are adding embellishments, remind them to keep items at the edge of the pillowcase so that they don't interfere with actually using the pillowcase comfortably!

Sewn Pillowcases
- Wash and press the fabric.
- Instruct teens on how to make the pillowcases.
    - Lay the fabric out, and using a pillowcase as a template, the dimensions of one as a guide, or one of the patterns found in the Resources section, cut the pieces, allowing for a seam allowance.
    - Sew the pieces together, hem, and press.
    - Add embellishments if desired.

RESOURCES

1 Million Pillowcase Challenge (patterns): www.allpeoplequilt.com/millionpillowcases/freepatterns

Instructables—How to Make a Simple Pillowcase: www.instructables.com/id/How-to-Make-a-Simple-Pillow-Case

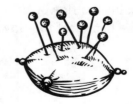

➡ Big Paper Blooms

Paper flowers may sound like a sad imitation of the real thing, but they are inexpensive and fun to make, and unlike those flowers bound by the laws of nature, they can be any color and size imaginable! And what's better—they will likely be welcomed into places where a little sunshine and brightness are desperately needed and live flowers are not allowed: cancer and transplant wards. Because of the potential for real plants (live or dried) to spread germs and fungus, they are not allowed in places where patients are severely immunocompromised. Individuals who have had a transplant or are undergoing chemo are often in the hospital for extended periods. Help to brighten their rooms *safely* with big paper blooms. Check with your local hospitals before embarking on this project to make sure that it adheres to their standards of care.

CROSSOVER

- Green Teens

SHOPPING LIST

Coffee Filter Flowers
- Coffee filters
- Floral wire
- Acrylic craft paint
- Green masking tape

Accordion-Fold Cut Paper Flowers
- Tissue paper
- Scissors
- Glue
- Fishing line or yarn

MAKE IT HAPPEN

Coffee Filter Flowers
- Fold the round coffee filter in half, then in half again.
- Trim the outer edge into a ruffle, fringe, or other design.
- Open the filter back up and insert a piece of floral wire through the center.
- Using the green tape, tape the base to the wire, twisting and tucking the paper as you go.
- Layer a few pieces this way to give the flower more fullness.
- Dilute the paint with water and either dip the edges of the flower into the paint and then invert it to let the paint drip down the paper, or use a paintbrush to paint the flower. If teens strive for realism, they can use darker tones toward the center of the flower.

Accordion-Fold Cut Paper Flowers

- Take two pieces of colorful tissue paper and fold each with an accordion fold, making two long, narrow rectangles.
- Fold each rectangle in half, making two short, narrow rectangles.
- Cut a design in the edges of one rectangle just as you might cut a paper snowflake. Do not cut all the way through and do not cut the fold.
- Place the cut piece on top of the uncut one and, with a pencil, mark the cuts that were made.
- Follow the pencil lines to make the same cuts.
- Open both papers up. Together they will form one whole flower.
- Place glue along the edges that will connect to form the whole. Place a piece of yarn or fishing line, long enough to run the length of the flower with enough remaining on one side to tie a loop, in the glue.

VARIATIONS

- There are lots of different ways to make paper flowers! See the Resources section for some ideas.

RESOURCES

Martha Stewart—How to Make Crepe-Paper Flowers: www.marthastewart.com/
893987/how-make-crepe-paper-flowers

Design Sponge—14 Paper Flower DIY Projects for Spring: www.designsponge.com/
2014/02/14-paper-flower-diy-projects-for-spring.html

Entertaining Teens

Training teens to develop entertainment skills serves a dual purpose for libraries. Teens may find a profitable passion they will enjoy throughout their lives, and libraries can harness those skills for inexpensive entertainment at library events! Performance techniques, overviews of entrepreneurship, and even public speaking polish can help a budding magician or promising politician.

POWER PROMOTION

- This club lends itself especially well to video clips. Showing snippets of meetings on library social media will highlight teens learning to juggle, becoming polished public speakers, and more, and it is hoped, inspire more teens to attend.
- After a few successful meetings where teens may learn to do some juggling or another entertaining skill, invite teens to perform at a library event.
- For example, they could do some juggling or host a puppet show for younger children at a National Library Week celebration. Have teens be prepared to mention their next meeting times at those occasions.

CROSSOVER PROGRAMS

- Photo and Video Blogs—Newsworthy Teens
- Promoting Yourself—Newsworthy Teens
- Deadline!—Newsworthy Teens
- Decades of Dance Moves—Active Teens

→ Taking the Fear Out of Public Speaking

Although speech class is required in many areas, it can only go so far in helping a teen who has to give a presentation at a job interview or speak at a professional conference for the first time. Getting up in front of a church group and persuading a library board to give money to a teen event are other instances when polished public speaking will be required of young people. A session on public speaking does not have to be dull or embarrassing. This program is designed to show teens that public speaking techniques can help them be their best and win their audience.

During this session, teens will learn how to Twitter-ize their introduction, points, and conclusion. They will also learn some relaxation and breathing techniques and give a one-minute persuasive speech. Interactive activities on things to avoid will make the session fun.

CROSSOVER

- Newsworthy Teens
- Author Event—Read-a-Latte Books and Media Club

SHOPPING LIST

- Pens and paper for notes, games
- Flip or phone camera if desired

MAKE IT HAPPEN

Instant Introductions: Have teens choose a partner and learn three or four facts about that person in one minute, then introduce the person to the rest of the room. When they are all finished, ask teens which facts they remember.

Best of Talks, Worst of Talks: Link to political or other speeches of a less-interesting nature and show a few short ones to the group. Then show an inspiring talk from history or a more recent one. A clip from a fund-raising telethon may be another example of a moving talk. Ask teens to note why the first clips were not interesting and why the latter one(s) worked.

Make It Stop: Invite volunteers from the group to give examples of bad techniques in public speaking—things that annoy them or make them stop listening.

Positively Persuasive: Ask the group to work in pairs to prepare a one-minute speech asking the library board for more money for digital equipment in a year when budgets are tight. Tape these and ask teens to evaluate themselves.

Just the Facts: The Newsworthy Teens Club in particular may enjoy this activity. Ask teens to list something that happened at school or in the local news in the last week and invite them to report on it in two hundred words or in one minute for a video camera. Did they cover the Who, What, Where, When, Why, and How? They can also interview an eyewitness (fictional for the purposes of the club) and tape that for evaluation.

Relaxation: Ask teens what helps them be less nervous about speaking in front of crowds. Have them do some stretching, deep breathing, and power posing and rate which are the most relaxing for them.

VARIATIONS

- The Volunteering and Community Service group (see the More Ideas for Established Clubs chapter) could work on the fund-raising pitches as a group project, with research and a presentation to be given to a board or administrators.
- Invite local speech team members from the high school to give tips and techniques from their competitions.

ONLINE

- Provide links to inspiring talks from history, either the words or video clips, on the library teen site, along with sites such as Toastmasters.
- Teens can post short news video clips on library business or club activities on the library teen social media sites.

RESOURCES

As most of the activities in this program relate to study of live performance, links are provided here.

American Rhetoric—Top 100 Speeches: www.americanrhetoric.com/top100speechesall.html

Teen Entrepreneur: http://teenentrepreneur.co.za/keeping-it-real

Toastmasters International: www.toastmasters.org

Van Petten, Vance Scott. *Ten Minutes to the Speech: Your Last-Minute Guide and Checklist for Speaking in Public.* Tallfellow Press, 2007.

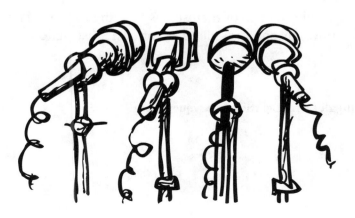

⬛➜ Just Juggling

Although juggling is a practice requiring dedicated study, the basics are easy to learn and can whet a teen's appetite for more information. Teens can then teach others or continue learning and juggle at library events, kids' parties, and other occasions. A fun, active practice, juggling can be enjoyed by any teen, even without skill.

CROSSOVER

- Active Teens

SHOPPING LIST

- Three small objects (such as apples, oranges, or beanbags) per teen
- Bouncing balls (such as tennis balls) for step 3
- Open plastic bags for step 4

MAKE IT HAPPEN

- Clear a space for practice and project the instructions and video clips.
- Show the basic instructions on the Learn How to Juggle website (http://learnhowtojuggle.info/getting-started) and work with teens through the steps.
- Try the bouncing off the wall activity with a few teens after watching this YouTube clip: www.youtube.com/watch?v=Acuaa8wFDsg.
- Watch this clip on learning to juggle in less than ten minutes and have teens try with open plastic bags rather than nylon scarves: www.youtube.com/watch?v=slOxPc4bAgs.
- Guest speaker: It would be fun to have a juggling performer show the teens some tricks or some more advanced techniques and discuss what kinds of places she performs at.
- If a guest speaker is not available, discuss what kinds of events jugglers may be hired for and what steps interested teens may take next. The teens in this group could teach kids in the youth department at a future event if they master the basics.

ONLINE

- Invite teens to submit clips of themselves juggling as they learn.
- Post how-to tutorials and provide links for basic instruction.

RESOURCES

International Jugglers' Association: www.juggle.org

→ Making Money from Entertainment

The teens in this club are learning some basic entertainment skills and ways to develop their talents into a business. This meeting will focus on the business end and help teens find and keep clients.

SHOPPING LIST

- No supplies need to be purchased for this meeting, though teens will want to look at websites or video clips as samples.
- Teens should have materials for taking notes on paper or electronically.

MAKE IT HAPPEN

Finding Potential Clients: If teens want to make money, discuss how they could be hired. Teens should ask friends, family members, and others in their circle if they would like someone to teach a craft at a kids' birthday party, for example. Discuss other places teens can find potential business, such as church events, park district programs, or library programs. The next step is professionally approaching potential clients.

Websites and Facebook Pages: Pull up websites of performers recently hired by the library or park district and ask teens how they could apply good qualities from these sites in a low-cost Facebook performer page or a website. What should they avoid?

Professionalism at Events: Explain that the key to gaining more clients is to do a good job with current ones.
- Checklist: Teens should develop a checklist of all supplies and steps needed for events.
- Teens under sixteen should be directed to state information about work permits.
- Budgeting: Do teens have money saved to purchase supplies and marketing materials before their first event? How could they earn it? Have them estimate what supplies will cost and what a reasonable fee may be.
- W-9s and Basic Tax Preparation and Accounting: Show teens a W-9 form and explain how income is reported on tax forms. If a W-9 is not provided by the person hiring the teen—for example, at a birthday party—the teen should report the payment as freelance income and should get advice from a tax professional.
- Mistakes: How should teens handle mistakes or things that go wrong? From an unhappy audience to a confused date, discuss scenarios and tactics to improve missteps. How should teens handle cancellations or problems collecting payment? Teens may want to work with a partner when starting out and should discuss the pros and cons of that situation.

Follow-Up and Client Retention, or Marketing 101: Discuss how clients should be thanked, either with written letters or mini gifts from the hired teen. How can teen performers develop newsletters? Many free newsletter websites exist.

Basic Business Cards or Clips: Give teens examples from performers or authors encountered by library staff and help them develop ideas for their own literature to hand out to potential clients. Teens may develop a flyer before spending money on business cards or having video clips made. This program will lead well to the Photo and Video Blogs session of the Newsworthy Teens Club as a way to advertise skills.

Other Streams of Revenue: Discuss other ways teens could earn money with the same skill in the future. If they do puppet shows at birthday parties, could they then teach kids how to make puppets? Could they do skits and face painting? Could they write articles or self-publish books on the subjects? Invite teens to start making a basic business plan.

SCORE Speakers: Invite speakers from local SCORE groups to talk to teens about resources they provide for small businesses.

VARIATIONS

- Entertainment Fair: Invite teens in the club or outside to showcase their skills at an event for party planners or other adults in the area to see. Teens can set up a booth or have a few minutes to perform in front of a drop-in audience of adults and children.

ONLINE

- Make a directory on the teen page with profiles of some teens and possible skills, as a virtual showcase.

RESOURCES

Brad Aronson—Teen Entrepreneurs: www.bradaronson.com/young-entrepreneurs
SCORE: www.score.org
Your Teen Business: www.yourteenbusiness.com

Improv 101

Improvisational skills are needed not only by people who aspire to star in sketch comedy shows. Improv teaches communication, team building, trust, and quick thinking, and is a whole lot of fun! If you have an improv troupe in your area, it's quite possible that someone will do a quick presentation and lead a few improv games at no charge, in exchange for promoting the organization. But even if you've never acted before, you will be able to lead teens through some fun and easy activities.

SHOPPING LIST

- Supplies will be minimal—a few chairs and a table should suffice.

MAKE IT HAPPEN

- Clear an area in your meeting room so there is plenty of space to move around.
- If you are concerned about teens being hesitant to suggest scenes or topics, prepare a few prompt cards to get the ball rolling.
- This program can be made up of a series of improv games. Consider some of the following.
  - The Alphabet Game: Given a prompt for a scene topic and a letter, the first player begins by using a word that begins with that letter. The other players must start their dialogue with each subsequent letter of the alphabet until they have wrapped all the way around the alphabet.
  - Mystery Date: With the "guesser" out of the room, three other players are given qualities or characteristics that they must embody. When the guesser comes back into the room, the scene unfolds as a dating game in which the guesser asks the other three people questions and then must guess their quirk.
  - Freeze Tag: Given a prompt for a scene, two or three teens begin acting it out. After some time, another teen shouts "Freeze!" and everyone on stage freezes. He then tags one player and takes her place, posing just as that player had been positioned. "Unfreeze" starts the action again, with the new player repeating the line that had just been spoken but taking it in a new direction.
  - Sounds Like Fun! This game begins with one person, but will eventually involve the whole group. The first person on stage says, "I think I'll [go grocery shopping, tie my shoes, put on makeup, have a dance party, etc.]" and then starts doing that action. The next person comes to the stage and says, "I think I'll . . ." and suggests a new action. The first player says, "Sounds like fun," and both do the action. This goes on, with everyone on stage saying "Sounds like fun" and joining the action until everyone is on stage participating.
  - One-Word Stories: The whole group tells a story only one word at a time. Ease into this by suggesting a well-known folk tale or popular story for them to tell.

RESOURCES

Improv Encyclopedia: http://improvencyclopedia.org

⬆ Open Mic Night

Give your entertaining teens a chance to try out their skills in front of an audience—even if it's just the members of the club. The open mic format is loose, low pressure, and supportive. An open mic brings together entertainers with a wide range of interests, from poets and classically trained musicians to novice jugglers and aspiring comedians—all are welcome. Cap off your programming year with this event or bring last year's group back at the beginning of the year with an open mic to encourage more teens to join.

SHOPPING LIST

- Depending on your venue, you may need nothing but chairs and a lectern or music stand.
- However, if you have a larger space or expect a bigger crowd, consider setting up a PA system with microphones and mic stands.
- If your library has a piano, by all means have the event in that room!
- Consider partnering with a local music shop to borrow or rent items like a PA system, microphones, mic stands, and a keyboard and stand.
- Offer refreshments to give the event a café feel.

MAKE IT HAPPEN

- Before the date of the event, begin promoting it to your teens, encouraging them to practice their material or partner with a friend to create a piece together.
- Ask if one or more teens want to emcee the event. This is great practice for teens who aspire to be comedians or who want practice talking in front of a crowd but don't especially care to perform otherwise.
- Promote outside the library at other venues with open mic nights, music stores, and "rock schools" and in the performing arts departments of your local schools.
- On the night of the event, set up the room with a stage area and small groupings of chairs with tables so teens can gather in friend groups.
- As teens arrive, you or your MC should greet them and have them check in as performers. Remind them of any guidelines you set, such as language and content restrictions and time limits.
- Thank everyone for coming, invite the performers up one at a time, sit back, and marvel at the talent in your community!

ONLINE

- Share the event online as it happens with Google Hangouts and consider taping the event (perhaps engaging Newsworthy Teens to practice their videography skills here) to broadcast on your library's YouTube channel.

➲ So Bad, It's Good Poetry Slam

Reading your own writing in front of an audience can be an intimidating task. This program seeks to break teens out of that mind-set by encouraging them to write, then perform, the worst poem possible.

SHOPPING LIST

- Notepads
- Pens

MAKE IT HAPPEN

- Share with teens some selected poems from the Alfred Joyce Kilmer Memorial Bad Poetry Contest (www.columbia.edu/cu/philo/kilmer) and encourage them to take a turn with dramatic readings of these poems.
- Talk about what makes bad poetry bad. Maybe it's having an overly simple rhyme, being too sentimental or emotional, using bad metaphors, or being totally nonsensical.
- Get writing! Encourage teens to write some bad poems and invite group input on how to make them worse.
- Dim the lights, don your beret, and stage your poetry slam with points assigned to the worst of the worst.

RESOURCES

Bynoe, Sara, ed. *Teen Angst: A Celebration of Really Bad Poetry*. St. Martin's Press, 2005.
The Worst Poems by Great Writers: www.telegraph.co.uk/culture/books/10651864/
The-worst-poems-by-great-writers.html

➡ Intro to DJ Skills

Whether teens aspire to delve into music production or to keep people dancing at the next weekend party, learning the basics of DJing will factor into their desired entertainment skills. For many teen librarians, leading this program will be a whole new experience. Consider using some of the techniques mentioned earlier in this book to find support to lead the program, either by calling on a teen or professional DJ to instruct or by learning right along with the teens. The following instructions will give you starting points for the latter.

CROSSOVER

- Technology Makers

SHOPPING LIST

- Computers or tablets (ideally one for each teen or pair of teens)
- Headphones
- A few different DJing apps (for example, VirtualDJ, djay 2, Traktor DJ, Pocket DJ Vintage)

MAKE IT HAPPEN

- After choosing a DJ app, load it onto the necessary devices and play around with it a bit. Learn where the controls are and where the Help function is and how to use it. In particular, explore how to transition from one song to the next.
- Search for video tutorials on the software you've chosen to share with the teens. The goal here is not to become an expert; rather, it is to know how to help teens find their own answers.
- Search also for some videos of professional DJs to inspire teens.
- Watch a few videos together, then set teens loose to see what they can learn and do. Use the "ask three, then me" method, whereby teens ask three of their peers before you step in to help solve their question. This isn't an avoidance technique! It encourages teens to take leadership roles and share their knowledge—which will in turn help them all learn more.

VARIATIONS

- Invite an instructor from a DJ school, community college, or local radio station, or a professional or amateur party DJ as a guest speaker.

ONLINE

- Extend the program by encouraging teens to share their mixes, successes, and tips with each other online.

RESOURCES

DJ Vocabulary: http://djtutorial.com/dj_glossary.htm
5 Basic DJ Transitions between 2 Songs: www.youtube.com/watch?v = rIsPx-8-_Is

Fashionista Teens

Many teens are exploring their identity and styles and may be looking for ideas. A club with a fashion focus can combine craft and art basics with tips and trends to inspire fashionistas.

POWER PROMOTION

- Promotions for this club can best use display space or good photos online.
- Samples of products or illustrations for projects for upcoming meetings should be prominently displayed in the library teen area or online.
- Invite teens to model projects from the club to inspire future members.
- After a year of club meetings, members may want to host their own fashion show or night featuring their work and inspiring others to join.

CROSSOVER PROGRAMS

- Travel Vision Board—Traveling Teens
- Sharpie T Chromatography—Scientific Teens

⮕ Polymer Food Charms

Polymer clay is an inexpensive medium that can easily be molded into attractive earrings or keychains by both beginner and advanced crafters.

CROSSOVER

- Food Fans

SHOPPING LIST

- Toaster oven(s) designated for baking clay (from thrift stores or garage sales, with at least two trays, and not used for food in the future)
- Polymer clay (such as Fimo) in an assortment of colors
- Long-nosed pliers (at least two sets)
- Wire cutters
- T-pins (for making earrings or attaching clay objects to keychains)
- Earring wires (ones with attached hinge backings are easiest and most useful)
- Keychain hardware
- Wooden dowel rods or implements to manipulate clay (optional; craft stores offer some, or improvised variations such as pencils may work as well)

MAKE IT HAPPEN

- Preheat the toaster oven.
- Show teens photos from books or online of creative items to be made from polymer clay. Etsy is a good source for these.
- Demonstrate how to take tiny amounts of clay to make earrings or slightly larger amounts for keychains (anything more than about 1-inch square will take too long to bake at a sixty- to ninety-minute club meeting).
- When teens finish their projects, pierce a hole through each item before putting the objects on a tray for baking.
- Bake a batch at a time for the length of time indicated on the package of clay.
- When objects are done, let them cool for a few minutes before putting the T-pin through.
- Use the pliers to wind the end of the pin around the earring or keychain hardware and bend the end in safely. Trim.
- While items are baking, ask teens for ideas for future meetings, or invite them to look through more fashion magazines or books.

VARIATIONS

- Food is not the only theme for polymer clay jewelry, though it is popular. This program can be offered with a Halloween or holiday theme, with teens making everything from pumpkins to stars.
- Teens can also create buttons, pins, charms, or beads with polymer clay, though larger projects may require more baking time.
- Teens can make different types of earrings while the clay is baking, such as simple bead creations.
- This meeting can be held over two sessions with the second meeting being devoted to painting and glitter finishes to further enhance the projects.

RESOURCES

Partain, Jessica, and Susan Partain. *The Polymer Clay Cookbook: Tiny Food Jewelry to Whip Up and Wear.* Potter Craft, 2009.

Scarr, Angie. *Miniature Food Masterclass: Materials and Techniques for Model-Makers.* Guild of Master Craftsman Publications, 2009.

Stowell, Charlotte. *Tasty Trinkets: Polymer Clay Food Jewellery.* Search Press, 2010.

YouTube Polymer Clay Tutorials: Many polymer clay food earring videos are available and can be linked to marketing for this meeting so teens can get ideas ahead of time.

⇨ Apron Decoration

Great for male or female teen chefs, or for gifts, aprons offer creative and practical canvases for inspiration.

CROSSOVER

- Food Fans
- Scrapbooking and Photography
- Crafting for Charity

SHOPPING LIST

- Blank canvas aprons (eBay often has lots of chef's aprons at bulk pricing; Oriental Trading Company has aprons to decorate as well)
- Sharpie markers in a variety of colors (both thick and thin tips)
- Protective table coverings
- Fabric paints (optional)
- Wipes, paper towels

MAKE IT HAPPEN

- Wash and press aprons as needed.
- Make samples or obtain photos for a PowerPoint presentation of different ways to decorate aprons. Ideas can include writing recipes for favorite foods, making colored dots by holding several Sharpies in one hand and covering the entire surface of the apron, drawing, and making borders.
- On the advertising for the program, note that decorations are permanent and that good clothing should not be worn to the meeting.
- Cover surfaces of tables.
- Set out the markers. If fabric paint is to be used, provide wipes and paper towels for quick cleanups.
- Go over ideas.
- Invite teens to decorate. If fabric paints are to be used, only a small area of the apron should be decorated as it will be hard to get the aprons home with paint on all parts without ruining the project or anything it touches.

Cupcakes

VARIATIONS

- Retro Aprons: Show photos of dressy and sheer midcentury aprons or other humorous past designs. Teens can be taught to hand sew or machine sew simple half-aprons with a gathered edge, ribbons, and hem tape out of gingham fabric or to apply ruffled trim to canvas aprons in vintage styles for a project that may extend for a few meetings.
- Crafting for Charity: Invite teens to wear decorated aprons to a shift at a local food pantry or a location that packages foods for hungry people. Or invite teens to design an apron for a raffle. Money donated will be given to that charity.
- Technology Inspired: Obtain iron-on transfer paper and use an inkjet printer to print food clip art or small pictures of teen food creations to add to the aprons. (Note: Small pictures transfer best.) Use an iron with no steam and be aware this process takes time.

RESOURCES

Craft Ideas to Decorate Kids' Aprons: www.ehow.com/info_7864062_ideas-decorating-kitchen-apron.html

Sharpie Pen Science: www.stevespanglerscience.com/lab/experiments/sharpie-pen-science

◨ Retro Fashions

Teens can try out and redesign popular crafts from past decades at this blast from the past.

CROSSOVER

- CREATEens
- Romantic Readers—Read-a-Latte Books and Media Club

SHOPPING LIST

Pom-poms
- Medium-weight yarn in assorted colors
- Scissors
- Cardboard sheets (cereal boxes work fine)
- Felt

Flower Power
- Flower looms (craft stores or thrift stores carry these)
- Medium-weight yarn in assorted colors
- Large plastic yarn needles
- Raffia ribbon (soft; optional)
- Barrette hardware (optional)
- Scissors (optional)

Woven Ribbon Barrettes
- ⅛-inch satin or grosgrain ribbon in assorted colors (two colors of 3 yards each per project)
- Metal bar barrettes with two parallel lines, either straight or wavy
- Light-weight beads (optional)
- Feathers (optional)
- Scissors (optional)

Macramé Bracelets
- Large safety pins
- Macramé thread or lighter weight crochet thread
- Clipboards (may be returned after project)
- Scissors

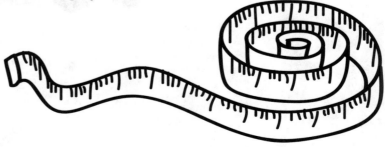

MAKE IT HAPPEN

- Find photos and variations for the four crafts online or in craft books (see Resources for starting points). Print directions for all four crafts with links in case members do not have a chance to try each craft. Some teens may want to spend all their time on one craft and try the others at home later. Teens may enjoy seeing how people wore these accessories. For example, find a photo of pom-poms tied on roller skates in the 1980s.
- Another option is to set up YouTube videos for the different crafts that teens can watch when they come in.
- Make at least one sample of each craft so you understand the directions.
- Set up four tables, each with the supplies for one craft.
- When teens arrive, go over the directions for all four crafts and let them choose which they would like to do. They can move from station to station or take supplies back to their spot, depending on room design.
  - Pom-poms: Show teens how pom-poms can be made by winding yarn around fingers, pulling off the loops, tying them across the middle, and cutting the loops. Larger pom-poms can be made using two cardboard C-shaped circles with a section cut. The outer circle can be smaller or larger but a 4-inch circumference is easy to work with. A circumference of 2 inches for the inner circle works well with the 4-inch circle. Yarn should be wound around the two pieces together so that no cardboard is showing. Slip scissors between the layers of cardboard to cut the yarn, and quickly tie a long string across the cut pieces to make a pom-pom. Teens may want to apply felt pieces to make pom-pom animals.
  - Flower Power: Find instructions online for particular flower looms or follow package directions, as they vary. All looms have string wound across the middle and ends in loops resembling a flower, and the string must be secured with stitches across the center (or in different stitches as long as it is secured) before being slid off the loom. These may be glued onto barrette hardware.
  - Woven Ribbon Barrettes: Demonstrate for teens how to hold two 3-yard lengths of ⅛-inch ribbon under the end of a metal barrette and weave them one at a time through the middle of the parallel bars to make V-shapes of color. When the weaving is finished, knot the ribbons underneath, leaving long strands of ribbon hanging down. Beads or feathers can be attached to the ends.
  - Macramé Bracelets: Basic macramé knot drawings can be found in library books or online. The basic friendship bracelet knot is also a form of macramé teens may find easy to duplicate.

VARIATIONS

- Themed Crafts: Retro crafts can be done in different colors for seasonal or holiday themes.
- In-Depth Crafting: If teens really enjoy a particular project, such as pom-poms, an entire week can be spent on it (for example, making pom-pom animals).

ONLINE

- Post links to directions, supplies, and videos for crafts each week and invite teens to post pictures of finished projects to the website.

RESOURCES

POM-POMS

5 Minute DIY—Yarn Pom Poms: www.youtube.com/watch?v = aTTDVryeFbY

How to Make a Yarn Pompom: www.wikihow.com/Make-a-Yarn-Pompom

Yarn Pom-Pom—Cardboard Circle Technique: www.youtube.com/watch?v = a03BTR3_3qg

FLOWER LOOM

Flowers Loom Tuts and More: www.pinterest.com/primative21/flowers-loom-tuts-ideas

The Hana-Ami Flower Loom Tutorial (uses the type typically found in craft stores): www.youtube
    .com/watch?v = vosN5aSWijs

How I Use a Flower Loom (instructions): www.pinkfluffywarrior.com/?p = 108

WOVEN RIBBON BARRETTE

Ribbon Braided Barrettes (tutorial): www.youtube.com/watch?v = Cyhegv8K-jY

MACRAMÉ

Basic Macramé Knots (directions): www.stonebrashcreative.com/MacrameTutorial.html

Three Ways to Make Hemp Bracelets: www.wikihow.com/make-hemp-bracelets

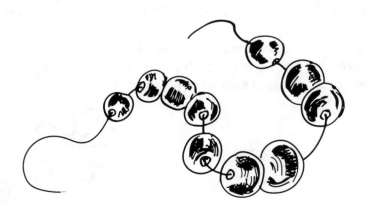

◘ Trashion Show

This program combines reusing recyclables and paper-pattern making with the fun of a design challenge. If you have access to old paper patterns (check your local thrift shops and ask your Friends of the Library group to keep their eyes peeled for patterns in the donation bins), bring them into the room for teens to cut apart and use as design pieces. If not, all you need is tissue paper or newspaper. This program can run with a challenge theme related to a specific event (prom dress, career wear, *Hunger Games* opening ceremony), cosplay interest, or a design requirement. The sky's the limit when it comes to the ways you can apply this program.

CROSSOVER

- Green Teens

SHOPPING LIST

- Paper patterns *or* tissue paper or tracing paper by the roll (can be purchased from artist supply stores) *or* newspapers
- Recyclables (bottle caps, egg cartons, six-pack rings . . . and any other items that your teens can collect and repurpose)
- Tape
- Markers and pencils
- Scissors
- Computer or tablet for browsing websites, fashion magazines, and design books for inspiration

MAKE IT HAPPEN

- Prepare your materials.
- Depending on the size of your group, have teens form teams or pairs.
- Instruct them on how a sewing pattern works.
  - Each piece that is a component of the garment is numbered and laid out on the paper.
  - To make the garment, cut the numbered pieces that are indicated along the correct size line and piece them together.
  - If teens were sewing a real garment, they would use the paper shapes here to cut fabric to sew together, but in this exercise, they will just be using the paper to get an idea of how patterns work and work quickly to create a garment.
- Introduce the design challenge that you have selected and give teens a time limit.
- Encourage teens to browse the patterns, design books, and any other fashion inspiration.

- Each group or pair now sketches the design that they want to make and gets to work cutting and taping their paper garment together and adding upcycled embellishments.
- At the end of the allotted time, host a fashion show with one teen modeling the garment and another discussing the various elements that were included in the design.
- Discuss challenges and triumphs that the teens encountered along the way. Talk about how it would be different to work with different types of fabric instead of paper.

VARIATIONS

- Focus on cosplay costumes for an anime club.
- Paper prototyping is a part of a lot of different maker projects. Introduce this to your Technology Makers to relate their projects to more traditional maker skills.
- Encourage your Green Teens to display the fashionable side of being environmentally friendly with the Trashion show.

ONLINE

- Again—this program will make for great photos!

RESOURCES

Newspaper Dress (Pinterest): www.pinterest.com/explore/newspaper-dress
Reading Pattern Symbols: www.sew-it-love-it.com/reading-patterns.html

◉ Ancient Fashions

Many of today's trends take their cue from ancient Greece, Rome, and Egypt. The Percy Jackson series of books has inspired interests in mythology, and teens may like to see modern takes on the ancient civilizations. This is a fun one to do around Olympic Games or Halloween times.

CROSSOVER

- Traveling Teens
- Romantic Readers—Read-a-Latte Books and Media Club

SHOPPING LIST

- Fashion magazines (staff may have extra copies at home that teens may cut up)
- Old sheets or fabric (thrift stores may have sheets; purple colors are best)
- White T-shirts (ask teens to bring these)
- Gold cording for belts
- Covered wire
- Laurel wreaths (craft shops may have something similar in silk florals)
- Wire cutters
- Scissors
- Tape
- Red ribbon

MAKE IT HAPPEN

- Pull books on ancient Greek myths or photographs of Greek temples with statues. Also, pull books on fashion history so teens can see examples. If this program is being offered for the Traveling Teens Club, show travel books for Greece, Rome, and Egypt featuring pictures of ruins and temples.
- Spread magazines out so teens can start finding examples of modern designs that draw from ancient looks. Ask teens what they would like to wear or design from ancient times.
- Show the How to Make a Toga and Laurel Wreath tutorial by the YES Magazine Project Crew: http://fashion.wonderhowto.com/how-to/make-toga-and-laurel -wreath-304516.
- Work with teens on making wreaths and togas.

VARIATIONS

- Toga Party: Conclude the meeting with a mini toga party where teens can eat figs, olives, grapes, or other snacks with Greek or Roman origins while wearing togas and wreaths.

ONLINE

- Post a link to the tutorial and invite teens to post pictures of their own toga or wreath creations.

RESOURCES

Many tutorials on making laurel wreaths or folding togas exist online. The **YES Magazine Project Crew** guys have a simple and fast tutorial (www.youtube.com/watch?v = ziuRtVUbjz8), but interested teens may enjoy more elaborate information and projects.

DIY Laurel Wreath Headband (fancy): www.youtube.com/watch?v = koy9vvNRwKk

How to Make a Toga out of a Bedsheet: www.wikihow.com/Make-a-Toga-out-of-a-Bedsheet

Toronto Star—How to Wear a Toga: https://www.youtube.com/watch?v = snUNFQwgTI4

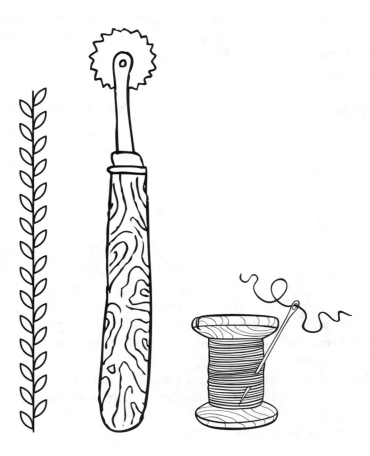

⮕ Simple Scarves

At this event, teens can learn to make two simple types of knitted scarves or knotted fleece scarves for themselves or groups in need.

CROSSOVER

- Crafting for Charity

SHOPPING LIST

Fleece Scarves
- ⅓ yard polar fleece per scarf
- Sharp fabric scissors
- Measuring tapes
- Chalk *or* removable fabric marking pen

Basic Knitted Scarf
- 2 skeins of Lion Brand Wool-Ease yarn per scarf (other medium worsted yarn will work)
- Pair of size 9 straight needles per scarf
- Scissors

Fancy Knitted Scarf
- 3–4 skeins novelty yarn per scarf (such as Lion Brand Fun Fur; *note*: novelty yarns are expensive but can be combined with plain yarn for effects)
- Knitting needles (likely size 10½ or higher as specified by yarn; straight needles)
- Measuring tapes
- Scissors

MAKE IT HAPPEN

- Pull fashion magazines (or ask staff to donate some) with photos of scarf trends.
- Pull basic knitting books as well as ideas on easy fancier scarves.
- Collect instructions for knotted polar fleece scarves.
- Cut ⅓-yard pieces so teens can select a project easily when they arrive.
- Invite teens to decide on groups to donate scarves to or discuss whether they want to auction fancier scarves for charity groups. They could also donate the scarves for local fund-raising auctions.
- Scarves may not get finished at this session, so give teens instructions and links for YouTube tutorials so they may finish at home, or invite them to bring projects back so staff can help them finish.

VARIATIONS

- Sewn Scarves: Crafty teens may want to use the sewing machine to make fancier polar fleece creations.

ONLINE

- Inspire teens by keeping a count of donated, finished projects and pictures on a website or Facebook page, along with links to directions and tutorials for further inspiration.

RESOURCES

18 Fleece Scarf Patterns and Tutorials (easy polar fleece scarves including no-sew):
    http://tipnut.com/fleece-scarf-patterns
Fun Fur Scarf: www.craftelf.com/Knitting_Fun_Fur_Scarf.htm
Knit a Garter Stitch Scarf: www.youtube.com/watch?v=p-WK7VveyqQ

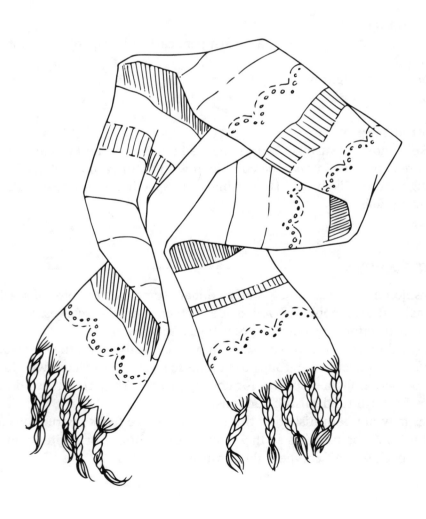

➡ Farewell Favorite Jeans!

The day will come for all of us—the day when our favorite jeans are worn out, stained, ripped, outgrown, or otherwise unwearable beyond our backyard. When that happens, what better way to remember a truly awesome companion than to turn those jeans into something you can keep forever? This program gives teens a chance to get creative by repurposing their favorite jeans into a tiny tote bag and a locker pocket.

CROSSOVER

- Scrapbooking and Photography

SHOPPING LIST

- Old jeans
- Scissors
- Needle and thread *or* sewing machines
- Measuring tapes
- Adhesive magnet strips
- Embellishments (ribbons, buttons, beads, sequins, etc.)

MAKE IT HAPPEN

Tiny Tote Bag

- The bag is made from the leg of the jean. The cuff becomes the bottom of the bag, and the straps will be made from the inseam and side seam.
- Teens should decide how deep they want their bag to be and how long they want the strap to be.
- Demonstrate how to add these two measurements together, then measure up from the cuff and cut off the jean leg.
- Instruct teens on how to make the bag.
  - Stitch the bottom of the bag closed. Teens can either turn the leg inside out to create a finished look or, to maintain the worn fringe that often develops on favorite jeans, sew straight across to use the fringed bits as embellishments.
  - Measure up from the new bottom of the bag and mark the top of the bag, and cut the front and back of the jeans away from the seams, leaving the seams connected to the bag.
  - Cut along the seams on either side, removing the pant leg from the seams.
  - Stitch or tie the top ends of the seams together to create a handle or shoulder strap for the bag.
  - Add embellishments.

Locker Pocket

- This project uses the back pockets of the jeans, so it should not interfere with the Tiny Tote Bag project if teens want to do both from one pair of jeans.
- Instruct teens on how to make the pocket.
  - Cut the back pockets away from the front of the jeans.
  - Trim the fabric into a shape that you like. It could be a simple outline or something more creative.
  - Affix adhesive magnet strips to the back of the pocket—what used to be the inside of the jeans.
  - Embellish the pocket with ribbons, patches, buttons, or other decorative accents.
  - Hang the pocket on the inside of a locker door to collect pens, spare change, notes, and the like—basically the same stuff teens put in there before the jeans' untimely demise!

VARIATIONS

- Use a high-quality fabric glue or heavy-duty fusible interfacing and an iron if your teens don't have access to sewing machines or don't want to stitch by hand.

RESOURCES

Allison, Scatha G., and Maria Stefanelli. *Jean Therapy: Denim Deconstruction for the Conscientious Crafter.* Quarry Books, 2008.

Blakeney, Faith, Justina Blakeney, and Ellen Schultz. *99 Ways to Cut, Sew and Deck Out Your Denim.* Potter Craft, 2007.

Flynn, Nancy. *Jeaneology: Crafty Ways to Reinvent Your Old Blues.* Zest Books, 2007.

→ T-Shirts to Scarves, Three Ways

Repurpose old T-shirts into fashionable scarves with these three easy techniques. If teens don't have T-shirts to use, you can easily pick some up at thrift shops. Look for shirts that are larger, have a good stretch, and are in fun colors.

CROSSOVER

- Green Teens

SHOPPING LIST

- T-shirts in a variety of colors
- Scissors
- Ruler
- Chalk
- Needle and thread

MAKE IT HAPPEN

Spiral Scarf
- Lay the shirt flat on the table.
- Cut off the arms, neck hole, and hem, leaving a rectangle.
- Starting from the outside edge, cut the shirt in a spiral design, all the way into the center of the shirt. Teens may want to draw this with chalk before cutting.
- Once teens have a cut spiral, they gently pull on the piece of fabric. This will ruffle the edges, leaving a twisty spiral scarf. Teens can cut more in different colors, tie them together, and experiment with different ways to wear the scarf.

Spaghetti Scarf
- Instruct teens to prep their T-shirt as for the Spiral Scarf so they have a rectangle.
- Cut strips of fabric perpendicular to the seamed edges, producing loops of fabric. Experiment with different widths.
- Once teens have the pieces they want, they should gently tug on the loops. This will curl the fabric so it will not fray. Teens can layer the pieces as desired, mix and match colors, try braiding some together, and style for wearing.

Arm Knit T-Shirt Scarf

- Have teens prep the shirt as above, but also cut along one side seam so that they have a long rectangle.
- Begin to cut the shirt into one long piece of fabric. Cut across, nearly to the edge, leaving about an inch. Move up to the next row and begin cutting on the opposite side, stopping again about an inch from the edge.
- Teens should continue alternating this cutting pattern until they have one long strip of fabric.
- An alternate method of cutting is to leave the shirt intact and, beginning at the bottom, cut an even width at an upward angle all around the shirt.
- Tug the edges and roll the fabric strip into a ball.
- Use fat knitting needles or an arm knitting technique to knit the T-shirt into an infinity cowl or chunky, loopy scarf.

VARIATIONS

- There are many different ways to craft a T-shirt scarf. See the Resources section.

RESOURCES

10 T-Shirt Scarf Tutorials: http://myblessedlife.net/2011/10/t-shirt-scarf-tutorial.html
Arm Knit T-Shirt Yarn Cowl: www.craftimism.com/2014/01/arm-knit-t-shirt-infnity-scarf.html
DIY T-Shirt Scarf: http://hellogiggles.com/diy-t-shirt-scarf

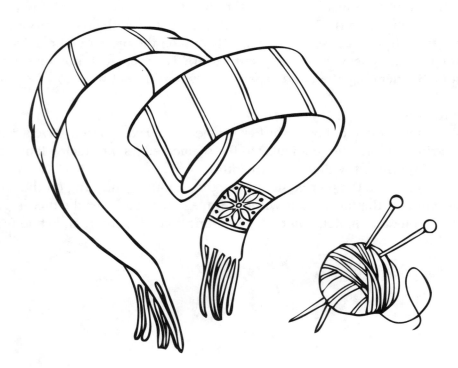

→ Flip-Flop Fix Up

A plain pair of flip-flops gets a makeover in this fun, warm weather craft. It's also a great way to get rid of small quantities of decorative items that you may have in the back of your craft closet—each pair of flip-flops requires only a few embellishments or a few feet of ribbon to get a whole new look.

SHOPPING LIST

- Assorted fabric ribbon
- Decorative beads, buttons, or gems
- Aleene's Tacky Glue, Beacon Flip-Flop Glue, E6000, or other strong multisurface adhesive (hot glue does not work for this craft)
- Flip-flops in assorted sizes and colors (or have teens bring their own)

MAKE IT HAPPEN

- Print out examples of several different styles of embellished flip-flops. Some wind ribbon around the thongs, others accent with gemstones, and still others use ribbon to fashion creative bows.
- Provide teens with the supplies needed to fancy up their own flip-flops.
- Advise teens on the correct use of the adhesive you have selected. Instructions will vary.

VARIATIONS

- Pair with a pedicure night to give teens who are painting their toes an activity that they can walk out in, without messing up their new polish.
- Stick to a theme with colors or embellishments: school colors, local team mascots, and pop culture tie-ins are fun options.

ONLINE

- This is a great project to show off online with a fancy flip-flop gallery.

RESOURCES

Embellished Flip-Flops: www.marthastewart.com/268565/embellished-flip-flops

Food Fans

Many teens—like adults—like to eat. This club celebrates food and helps teens tie food to health, creativity, and even careers.

POWER PROMOTION

- Food programs often need little promotion to attract patrons.
- Large photographs of food on posters or online will gain attention, as will the scent of food at the events.
- Program names that clearly state that food is involved will help promote this group.
- Program information could also be put on cards with a recipe on the back for a smoothie or other health-conscious, teen-appealing food.

CROSSOVER PROGRAMS

- Apron Decoration—Fashionista Teens
- Polymer Food Charms—Fashionista Teens
- Recipe Scrapbooking—Scrapbooking and Photography
- Smoothie Station—Active Teens

→ Baking Basics

Sometimes, reading about food isn't enough, and teens want to get their hands dirty learning something new. Like a big, messy food maker program, Baking Basics allows teens to handle eggs, create pie crusts, and make a basic refrigerator cake.

CROSSOVER

- Scientific Teens

SHOPPING LIST

- Large mixing bowls (2 per group of 4 teens)
- Parchment paper
- Table coverings
- Pastry cutters (1 per group)
- Rolling pins (1 per group; large cans will also work)
- Whisks (1 per group)
- Measuring container for water
- Eggs (2 per teen)
- Sticks of shortening (1 per group)
- Flour (1 large bag will cover program)
- Canned frosting (1 per group, any flavor, but do not get easy spreading or extra smooth)
- Large, soft chocolate chip or sugar cookies (2 per teen)
- Hand sanitizer and wipes
- Garbage bags
- Plastic knives
- Small paper plates
- Baggies
- Tupperware container for cleanup

MAKE IT HAPPEN

- As teens come in, invite them to use the hand sanitizer.
- Go over some safety and health guidelines for baking (see Resources).

Pie Crust

- Guide teens through mixing basic pie crust with the following recipe:
  - 1 cup flour
  - ⅓ cup plus 1 tablespoon vegetable shortening
  - 2–2½ tablespoons cold water
  - Combine ingredients except water. Use pastry cutter and add water as the dough starts to come together. Take ball of dough and roll it out on a lightly floured surface until the crust is large enough for an 8- or 9-inch pie pan.
- Once they have rolled out the crust on the parchment paper, they can throw it out and get ready for the next activity.

Egg Technique

- Show teens how to crack eggs against the side of the bowl. They may each practice with two, then practice whisking for a few minutes. The teens in a group can share the bowl and take turns whisking.
- Teens can then dump the mixture into the Tupperware container, stack the bowls, and wash or sanitize their hands again.

Refrigerator Cake

- Instruct teens to frost the top of one of their cookies and place the other on top. Then they will cut the stacked cookies in half and stack them again, making four layers of a mini refrigerator cake. Teens may eat their creations or take them home.

VARIATIONS

- A library with time and resources can provide pie plates and canned pie filling and bake the pies, showing the finishing details. Teens can eat their creations.

RESOURCES

Measuring Ingredients: www.dummies.com/how-to/content/measuring-ingredients-for
   -baking.html
Ten Baking Safety Checks: www.homebaking.org/foreducators/mmandbprogram.html

➡ Teen Tasters

Trying out variations of favorite foods is fun in this sampling and voting program. To cut expenses, offer smaller samples or fewer choices. This topic may develop into its own club, and sessions could run around forty-five minutes.

SHOPPING LIST

- 10 variations on a food theme (for example, a Scary Treats theme in October could have different flavors of Halloween candy, pumpkin items, and apple-flavored doughnuts; doughnuts, potato chips, fruits and dips, chocolate, breads, drinks, snack cakes, and more could work as themes.)
- Plates
- Plastic baggies

MAKE IT HAPPEN

- Provide paper and pencils for teens to make notes and vote on samples.
- Begin serving treats and encourage discussion of each.
- Teens can vote on favorites periodically.
- Teens should be encouraged to taste each sample and put the remainder in the baggies to finish at home.

VARIATIONS

- Invite teens to come up with future taster foods. Have some holiday-themed or generic ones also to get them to try new things.
- Retro Favorites: Serve long-loved snacks such as MoonPies and discuss the history behind each sample.

ONLINE

- Putting up links to favorite food companies or restaurants and allowing for teen voting are two ways to keep momentum on this topic going.

⮞ Spice It Up!

What's the difference between coriander and cumin? Did you know chipotle isn't just a restaurant—it's a pepper, too? This event allows teens to taste, smell, and see a variety of spices that they may be unfamiliar with.

CROSSOVER

- Traveling Teens

SHOPPING LIST

- Napkins
- Plastic utensils
- Small paper cups (for presenting seasonings)
- Olive oil
- Bread
- A variety of spices and seasonings (Pull from your own cabinet at home, or visit a local bulk food store to purchase small quantities for better prices. Consider the following.)

The Basics

- Basil
- Dill
- Oregano
- Parsley
- Rosemary
- Sage
- Thyme

A Bit More Sophisticated

- Cumin
- Curry powder
- Chipotle
- Herbs de Provence
- Lavender
- Savory
- Turmeric

MAKE IT HAPPEN

- Purchase the spices you plan to use.
- Set out cups with a small amount of olive oil and some seasoning in each container. Place each cup on a piece of paper with the name of the seasoning.
- Cube the bread and set out baskets at each tasting station.
- Talk about the five tastes: salty, sour, sweet, bitter, and umami (see Resources).
- Encourage teens to smell each herb or spice before tasting it.
- Teens can cycle through the stations and sample each spice by spreading a small quantity on a bread cube. Give teens paper for taking notes. Offer a "spice glossary" with photos to help them describe the flavors they experience.

VARIATIONS

- Focus on common spices and seasonings from various regions of the world.
- Focus on spices used with specific types of cooking (those used in baking, those used in grilling, those used in soups, etc.).
- Repeat the program with a variety of hot sauces.
- Include recipes that feature each type of herb or spice for take-home extensions.
- Invite a local chef to discuss or demonstrate how he or she pairs spices and seasonings with different foods.

ONLINE

- Invite teens to share their flavor explorations online, either with recipe exchanges or reviews.

RESOURCES

Adjectives for Describing Foods: www.thefoodies.org/images/Adjectives%20for%20 describing%20foods.pdf

McCormick Spices: www.mccormick.com/Spices-and-Flavors/Herbs-and-Spices/Spices

McGee, Harold. *On Food and Cooking: The Science and Lore of the Kitchen.* Scribner, 2004.

→ Extreme Gingerbread

Teens use graham crackers and candy to create "gingerbread" structures. This is a messy and time-consuming program, but the fun is worth the effort. There are a number of ways to run this program. It easily fits in with several holiday celebrations—Christmas and Halloween are natural fits. But you could also structure it as a book-related activity, encouraging teens to re-create a building or scene from a book or a home for a favorite character. Set up an engineering design challenge to cross over with Technology Makers, or set teens on task to design an ecofriendly building as an activity for Green Teens. If your library has display space, these creations are an awesome item to display and proudly show off the creativity of your teens.

CROSSOVER

- Green Teens
- Read-a-Latte Books and Media Club
- Scientific Teens
- Technology Makers
- Traveling Teens

SHOPPING LIST

- Graham crackers
- Royal icing (this is not icing in a can—it is the glue that will hold the structures together)
- Sturdy ziplock plastic bags
- Table covers
- Plastic knives
- Assorted candy, cereal, and other foods (to use in decorating and accessorizing the structures; save money by collecting unwanted Halloween candy to use at a later date, or ask each teen to bring one item to use in the program)

MAKE IT HAPPEN

- Decide on your challenge. It could be a holiday theme, a building theme, or a theme limited by materials.
- Prepare the room:
  - Cover the tables.
  - Open the graham crackers and make sure too many aren't broken.
  - Divide the royal icing into the ziplock bags.
  - Set out the decorations and embellishments.
  - Cut cardboard into pieces for each teen to have a building base.
- Allow teens time to build, judge (if structured as a contest), and clean up.

VARIATIONS

- For Green Teens—challenge them to create an ecofriendly building.
- For Traveling Teens—encourage them to re-create a world-famous building or structure.
- For Scientific Teens—use this as a prototyping activity or incorporate lights or sounds by applying the concepts learned in the Squishy Circuits program.

RESOURCES

Extreme Gingerbread Challenge: www.teenlibrariantoolbox.com/2012/12/tpib-extreme -gingerbread-challenge

→ Cake Decorating Basics

You never know when someone's going to need a custom cake! In this program, teens will learn the basics of cake decorating by trying out a variety of icing tips and techniques. Use cereal boxes as decorating bases to save time and funds by skipping real cake and focusing on the decorating.

CROSSOVER

- Crafting for Charity

SHOPPING LIST

- Premade icing
- Food coloring
- A variety of cake decorating tips (can be purchased at the grocery store)
- Ziplock bags
- Plastic knives
- Plastic table covers
- Cardboard boxes (to use as decorating bases)
- A handout on icing tips (see Resources)
- Paper towels
- Photos of cakes to illustrate different techniques

MAKE IT HAPPEN

- Prepare your space: cover the tables and set out paper towels, cake photos, and handouts on icing tips.
- Prepare your supplies:
  - Snip the corner of a plastic bag and drop a tip in. Fill the bag with icing and close it. Prepare one bag per tip style for each group, ensuring that there are enough bags for each teen to have one at all times.
  - Give each teen or group of teens a box. If the exterior is printed, like a cereal box, have them take it apart and turn it inside out so that the plain cardboard is showing.
  - Give each teen or group of teens a set of icing bags with the pre-placed tips. Have the teens experiment with the different tips and discover the different types of lines or decorations that each makes.

VARIATIONS

- Decorate cookies.
- Tie in with a holiday.
- Use real cakes or cookies and donate them to a nursing home, homeless shelter, fire station, or the like.

ONLINE

- Post photos of the creations! Have fun even with the creations that didn't turn out so well with a Nailed It/Failed It Pinterest board.

RESOURCES

Decorating Bag Tips: www.wilton.com/decorating/decorating-basics/decorating_tips.cfm

⬡ Chocolate Chip Cookie Science

They say that cooking is an art, but baking is a science. Teens can use the tools and knowledge learned in the Baking Basics program to expand on that maxim. In this program, each teen or group takes the basic chocolate chip cookie recipe, tweaks it slightly, and compares the results.

CROSSOVER

- Scientific Teens

SHOPPING LIST

- Chocolate chips
- Flour (can use different types of flour)
- White sugar
- Brown sugar
- Eggs *or* liquid egg substitute
- Shortening *or* butter
- Vanilla extract
- Baking soda
- Baking powder
- Nonstick spray
- Plastic spoons
- Paper *or* plastic bowls
- Paper towels
- Plastic table covers
- Measuring cups and spoons
- Foil
- Cookie sheets
- Parchment paper
- Oven *or* toaster oven
- Hot pads
- Spatula
- Sharpie
- Small-batch cookie recipe (see Resources)

MAKE IT HAPPEN

- Prepare a batch of cookies from the recipe you'll be providing to the teens.
- Prepare your space: cover the tables, set out ingredients and measuring tools. Cut foil sheets and parchment paper to size and use the Sharpie to make a grid on each. Number the grid spaces on each.
- Talk to the teens about the test kitchen concept: take a recipe, change one thing, and see what results. Give them each a cookie to taste test, then give them the recipe, ask them to decide what to change, and have them write it down. Encourage scientific thinking by asking them to make a prediction about what will happen. Then bake away! When each teen or group finishes, have them place their cookie batter onto the foil-covered cookie sheets and make note of the grid spaces they use.
- Once the first batch is done, remove the cookies to the parchment paper, keeping them in the same grid spaces. Have a taste test and see how the adjustments made impact the resulting cookie. If there's still time, have teens do another iteration of their recipe.

VARIATIONS

- This activity doesn't need to be done with chocolate chip cookies—you could use any number of other recipes. If you have kitchen space, try a chili cook-off. If you don't have access to a toaster oven, try variations of no-bake cookies. If you just have a microwave, do variations of mug cakes. The possibilities are endless!

ONLINE

- Use a baking calculator to scale the recipes back up to a normal yield and share the best recipes created online!
- A great number of food bloggers have posted about the process they used to arrive at their "perfect" chocolate chip cookie. Sharing some of these with teens may set them on the right course.

RESOURCES

Maugans, Debby. *Small-Batch Baking for Chocolate Lovers.* St. Martin's, 2011.
My Kitchen Calculator: www.mykitchencalculator.com

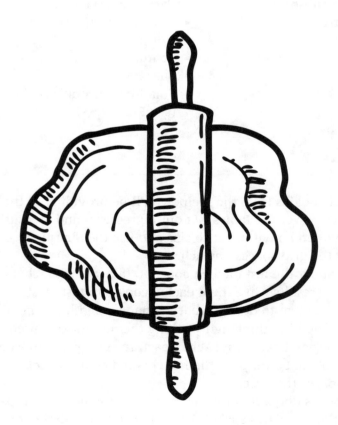

→ Designer Hot Cocoa

When the weather turns cold, nothing beats curling up with a nice cup of hot cocoa. This program invites teens to try something different by concocting their own signature cocoa recipe. The easiest way to do it is to purchase a cocoa mix and offer a variety of flavors to add in. But for teens who really get a thrill out of creating from scratch, try the old-fashioned cocoa powder method!

CROSSOVER

- Crafting for Charity

SHOPPING LIST

- Instant coffee powder
- Vanilla extract
- Cinnamon
- Cayenne pepper
- Mint extract *or* crushed peppermints *or* crushed candy canes
- Mini marshmallows
- Oreos (crushed)
- Chocolate bar (use a vegetable peeler to make chocolate curls)
- Other assorted mix-ins (colored sugar, sprinkles, additional flavor extracts)
- Ziplock bags *or* decorative storage containers
- Address labels
- Pens *or* Sharpie markers
- Hot/cold cups
- Plastic spoons
- Just-add-water hot cocoa mix *or* cocoa powder
- Powdered sugar
- Nonfat dry milk powder

MAKE IT HAPPEN

- Prep your space: cover tables, set out containers for teens to fill, set out ingredients and spoons.
- Heat some water if you'll be encouraging teens to test their recipes during the program.
- Provide the list of cocoa recipes and paper for teens to write down their own.
- Have teens create their cocoa recipes and label them with creative names.
- If using sugar, cocoa powder, and dry milk, follow the ratio of 2:1:2½.

Recipes

THE OLD FASHIONED
- Basic mix

THE RUDOLPH
- Basic mix
- Mint extract *or* crushed peppermints *or* crushed candy canes
- Marshmallows

THE VIXEN
- Basic mix
- Mint extract *or* crushed peppermints *or* crushed candy canes
- Dash of cayenne pepper
- Dash of cinnamon
- Marshmallows

THE CAMPFIRE
- Basic mix
- Marshmallows

THE SOUTH-OF-THE-BORDER
- Basic mix
- Cinnamon
- Dash of cayenne pepper

THE EIFFEL TOWER
- Basic mix
- Instant coffee powder
- Chocolate curls

THE COOKIES 'N' CREAM
- Basic mix
- Crushed Oreos
- Marshmallows

THE SWEET TOOTH
- Basic mix
- Mint extract *or* crushed peppermints *or* crushed candy canes
- Chocolate curls
- Crushed Oreos
- Marshmallows

THE ALL-NIGHTER
- Basic mix
- Instant coffee powder
- Marshmallows

VARIATIONS

- Structure this as a gift-making program and fancy up the containers with scrapbook stickers or ribbons.
- Donate gift-quality products to charity locations, such as homeless shelters or nursing homes.

Game On

Teens are so busy these days, it's hard to find the time to step back and just have some fun. The Game On Club is a way to schedule some fun, relaxing, gaming time into teens' busy lives. Gamers are a dedicated and devoted bunch. Although your community may have a group of die-hard Magic players and another group that lives and dies by Madden and still another with a regular D&D campaign, this club strives to bring them all together in their love of gaming for some shared fun and idea swapping. Additionally, this club will appeal to teens who are just looking for a fun outlet. Individual club meetings on various topics may appeal more to some than to others and may be an effective way to bring new people in.

As you look into games to use in this club, local game shop owners can be excellent resources and would make great guest speakers periodically. The gaming community online is another place to turn for help, with sites like Board Game Geek (http://boardgamegeek.com) being a great way to get reviews of games, find missing rules, and get tips on fun game play.

POWER PROMOTION

- If your library circulates games of any kind—board games, video games, and so on—use them in your promotion by inserting small ads designed to look like game cards into the packaging.
- Seek out the spots in town that draw gamers and post flyers. Game stores, toy stores, comic shops, book stores and restaurants and hangouts with game nights, and school clubs for gamers are places to consider.

- Set up a game table in the teen area festooned with advertisements for the club. Put out a chess board, a puzzle, a board game, or other games that require little setup like Apples to Apples or Catchphrase. If you see teens playing, ask if you can join their game for a round and talk up the club.
- Turn attendance at club meetings into a game of its own with a board game–style punch card that can be redeemed for prizes or drawings.
- Before starting the club, consider soliciting game donations in your library's newsletter. Chances are there are families in your community who have discovered they have no love for some of their games or have aged out of others. This is a great way to collect old favorites and get your hands on obscure and off-the-wall games that you've never even heard of.

CROSSOVER PROGRAMS

- Active Inner Child—Active Teens
- Fantastic Readers—Read-a-Latte Books and Media Club
- Geocaching—Scientific Teens
- Improv 101—Entertaining Teens
- Just Juggling—Entertaining Teens
- Reuse–Remake–Renew—Green Teens

⮊ Board Game Speed Dating

This is a great way to start your club. Everyone has an opportunity to try out a whole bunch of old favorites or new-to-you games in quick succession. It's also a good mixer for teens who may not yet know each other.

SHOPPING LIST

- Games (You will need a variety—at least 4 for a one-hour program. Call on community members, library staff, or local game shops for game donations or ask to borrow them for this event.)
- Paper (for players to take notes)
- Pens, pencils

MAKE IT HAPPEN

- Set up the room with a different game on each table and the correct number of chairs for each game.
- When teens arrive, assign them to a table or group.
- Quickly go over the basic game play for each activity and explain that teens will be rotating to a new game every ten or fifteen minutes.
- Provide review sheets for teens to jot down notes on how they like each game they play.
- Rotate through the games, calling "Time!" when they need to switch.
- Before the program ends, collect review sheets and chat about which games were the most fun to play, which they would like to see again, and which could safely go in the used book sale.

VARIATIONS

- Focus on one specific type of game—say, German board games, games with role-play elements, word games, and so on.
- Scramble the teams each time you rotate games to make this more of a mixer.
- Have teens bring their favorite games and allow each to introduce his own game or host the play throughout the evening.

ONLINE

- With no lack of online games to play, you could provide a list or links to popular online games, invite teens to try them out, and then give feedback or reviews.

⮕ *Go Fish* under the *Bridge* before the *President Goes* to *War*

Everyone knows at least one or two card games. A deck of cards is compact and inexpensive, and many card games are easy to pick up and remember how to play, making card games a nice way to bring people together in an activity on the spur of the moment. In this program, delve deeper into card gaming by selecting a game that teens don't yet know and let them work on perfecting their game over the hour.

SHOPPING LIST

- Standard decks of cards

MAKE IT HAPPEN

- Set up the room with tables for four to six people, depending on the game you are going to learn.
- There are so many to choose from! Gauge your selection by the temperament of your group. If your teens have a hefty attention span and an interest in bidding and partner games, consider introducing bridge or whist. If they tend toward more joviality, find something that plays on that like Spoons or President. Here are some easy games to consider:
  - I Doubt It: The dealer deals all the cards. It doesn't matter if it comes out uneven. The game play proceeds clockwise. Each person puts a card or cards face down in the center of the table, stating what she is placing down (for example, "two jacks, one four"). If someone doubts that this is true, the cards must be flipped over. If the player was telling the truth, the doubter must take the whole pile of cards. If the player was lying, she must take the whole pile. The winner is the first to play all of her cards.
  - Spoons: This game requires spoons—one less than the number of players. The goal is to collect four of a kind. The dealer deals four cards to each player. Then the dealer takes the top card from the deck, decides whether or not to keep it, and discards clockwise. Then the dealer draws another card as the person to his left is examining and discarding, with all players picking up and discarding simultaneously. As soon as a player has four of a kind, she discreetly grabs a spoon from the center of the table and continues to pass cards. This person is the winner. As soon as others notice this, they also take spoons, leaving the last person without. That person is the new dealer.

- Hearts: This is a card-passing game for four, where the goal is to end the game with no points by avoiding all hearts and the queen of spades.
- Here are some more complicated games to look up (see Resources):
  - Euchre: This is a partner game with tricks, played by four people with a partial deck.
  - Whist: A fixed partner game with tricks, this game is called a simplified bridge by some. The rules are simple, but the game play allows lots of room to expand and think critically about strategy.
  - Poker variations: This betting game (use candy, beads, or pennies) can be played numerous ways with a range of players.
  - Tripoli (Michigan Rummy): This is a three-stage game that involves betting and a board, which can be easily re-created with paper and markers.

RESOURCES

Gibson, Walter B. *Hoyle's Modern Encyclopedia of Card Games: Rules of All the Basic Games and Popular Variations.* Three Rivers Press, 2013.

Pagat's Card Game Rules—Card Games and Tile Games from around the World: www.pagat.com

The Official Rules According to Hoyle: www.hoylegaming.com/rules

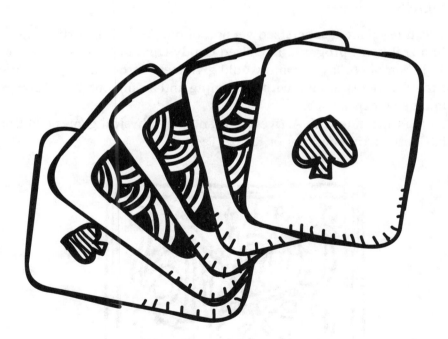

⮕ Flashback Game Night

Gaming teens love to play, we know that. Hosting a flashback game night will remind them of how much they've *always* loved to play. It's also a good way to bring in new members who will have fun with the nostalgia of a game night like they might remember from childhood.

SHOPPING LIST

- Childhood games (Operation, Hungry Hungry Hippos, Memory, Candy Land, and so on)
- Refreshments (optional; animal crackers, applesauce, fruit roll-ups, and the like)

MAKE IT HAPPEN

- Encourage teens to get comfy—take off shoes, sit on carpet squares, maybe even put on some kids' music!
- Have a fun and relaxing evening playing these childhood games. Chat about which ones are still fun. Ask if any are different than teens remember.

VARIATIONS

- Teens can re-create a supersized version of one of their favorite games to use in a children's program. Life-sized Candy Land or Chutes and Ladders would be simple to lay out and would give teens a role in helping. Enlist Entertaining Teens to help with costuming and acting out parts to give kids an immersive experience.
- Host a joint meeting with Active Teens and play physical games like Duck, Duck, Goose or Human Knot or Freeze Tag.

⮕ Mashup Your "Bored" Games

Did you used to love playing Sorry? Has Monopoly lost its luster? Has Trouble been a bother since some pieces got lost down the heating vent? This program gives teens a chance to revamp their tired "bored" games by swapping pieces, rewriting rules, and reinventing the game play into something that's fun again! Invite teens to bring their own "bored" games, solicit donations from library staff and patrons, or buy them on the cheap at resale shops.

CROSSOVER

- Reuse–Remake–Renew—Green Teens

SHOPPING LIST

- Board games (it doesn't matter if they are complete)
- Markers
- Card stock
- Scissors
- Beads, clay, or other craft supplies (to use to make new playing pieces)

MAKE IT HAPPEN

- Collect your games and game-making supplies.
- Invite teens to work in groups to invent some new games based on the pieces available.
- Make new pieces, playing cards, or other necessary items.
- Encourage teens to write rules for their new game and give it a name.
- Invite teens to doctor the box to reflect the game's new life!

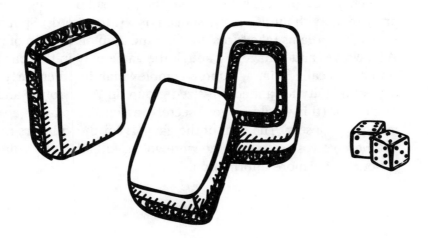

⮕ Social Games

Social, or party, games are those that can be played with larger groups of people, are easy to start playing, and focus more on interaction among players than on the plot of a game. This type of gaming is nice because it's an inclusive way to interact around a game and can be a great icebreaker in social situations.

SHOPPING LIST

- Note pads and paper
- Wipe-off board *or* large paper pad

MAKE IT HAPPEN

- Talk to teens about the function of social games. They can be mixers at parties, an inexpensive way to have fun with friends without going out, or a way to get to know people better. Point out that learning a few social games will come in handy, as they will inevitably pop up in adulthood in the form of mixers at engagement parties, baby showers, and similar gatherings of people who don't all know one another.
- Ask teens for their favorite social games and select a few to play. Here are some to consider:
  - Charades: This is perhaps the classic party game. Split the group into two teams. Each person thinks up an idea to be acted out by the opposite team and writes it on a slip of paper. You could limit it to a theme like movies, holidays, people in the news, or teen books, or it could just be a free-for-all. Everyone gets a chance to draw a slip and act it out without using any words. Only players on the actor's team should try to guess. Charades does allow for plenty of signals to indicate different ideas or words, and a list of some signals can be found online (see Resources).
  - Pictionary: You don't need to purchase the board game to play this game. As with charades, players submit ideas, but instead of acting them out, players draw them without using any spoken or written words. Split the group into two teams. Teams take turns drawing the item on the slip of paper.
  - Werewolves and Villagers: Though the game play in this party game, sometimes called Mafia, is more complex than in other party games, it's a great activity for a medium-sized group. In Werewolves and Villagers, a moderator (this would be you) secretly assigns all players a role: werewolf, villager, or a seer. The goal of the game is for the villagers to detect who the werewolves are before the werewolves kill all of the villagers. See Resources for more information.

- Categories: If you've played Scattergories, you can play Categories. In this game, first a match word is decided upon—*read, game, library*—and then a category is named. The category could be anything—movie stars, song titles, states, kitchen tools, sports teams, YA authors—anything of which there are plenty of items to choose from. Everyone then tries to list something from each category that begins with each letter of the match word. For example, using the match word *game* and the category of YA authors, players could say, "Michael Grant, Laurie Halse Anderson, Tahereh Mafi, and E. Lockhart." Points are assigned for items that do not appear on anyone else's list, and players can dispute whether any item can actually count (for example, "E. Lockhart" could be disputed in the preceding example because it's not a last name that begins with the designated letter).
- Two Truths and a Lie: This is a classic icebreaker that gets harder the more you know the group you're playing with. In it, each person writes down two true things about himself and one lie. The goal is to detect which item is a lie.

RESOURCES

Charades Signals: www.outsetmedia.com/charadessignals

How to Play Werewolf (Werewolves and Villagers instructions): www.brenbarn.net/werewolf/rules.html

Ragsdale, Susan, and Ann Saylor. *Great Group Games: 175 Boredom-Busting, Zero-Prep Team Builders for All Ages.* Search Institute Press, 2007.

→ What's New in Games?

Once your teens have tackled their favorites and had some fun, the spark will have been lit. Fuel that fire by hosting a program where teens can find out about all the latest and greatest. If you have a local game shop, invite the owner to be a guest speaker. This is great promotion for the shop as everyone in attendance will already be a gaming fan! If you are in an area without a gaming store, there are still lots of ways to find out about new games.

SHOPPING LIST

- New games (either purchased based on recommendations or as loaners from a game shop—ask to borrow demo copies)
- Game catalogs and magazines
- Computers with Internet access

MAKE IT HAPPEN

There are a number of ways to run this program:
- Ideally, this will function as a program with a guest speaker—your gaming expert from a local game shop, who will bring demo copies of games for teens to play.
- If there is no guest speaker to invite, present the program yourself. Try borrowing games from library patrons who are into gaming, requesting new games that circulate in your library system, or purchasing a few up-and-coming games to try out.

Break this into a two-phase program.
- In phase one, teens will need computers and toy and game catalogs.
- Browse together to find new games (see Resources) and read reviews.
- Discuss which games sound like the most fun and the best fit for the club. Consider the budget that the library has to spend on teen programming and the amount that the teens would be allowed to request for additions.
- After they have made their decisions, order the game or games that the teens have recommended.
- Phase two is to play the new games! Consider asking teens to write reviews of the games to post on your blog or on game review sites.

VARIATIONS

- If your community or region has a toy and game fair, take a field trip to explore it.

ONLINE

- Seek out game companies online via Twitter. Consider contacting them for review copies of new games or ask their recommendations for their biggest picks for the season.
- Plenty of vloggers review games, too. Find them on YouTube and have a review watching party before ordering new games.

RESOURCES

BoardGaming: http://boardgaming.com

Casual Game Insider: http://casualgamerevolution.com/magazine

Friendly Local Game Stores of the USA: http://boardgamegeek.com/wiki/page/
    Friendly_Local_Game_Stores_%28FLGS%29_of_the_USA

Shut Up and Sit Down: www.shutupandsitdown.com

TAGIE Awards (Toy and Game Inventor Awards): www.tagieawards.com/award-history

→ Speed Puzzle Challenge

Are puzzles really games? If you don't think so, add a competitive edge and your mind will be changed! This program is great to get some friendly competition going. Teens can compete with each other individually or on teams. While choosing puzzles, try to rank them in terms of difficulty, not just piece count. For example, a 500-piece puzzle with lots of color and different shapes is not going to be as difficult as a 500-piece puzzle that shows a minimalist snow scene. A double-sided puzzle, a 3-D puzzle, or a mystery puzzle will be more difficult than a traditional one.

SHOPPING LIST

- Jigsaw puzzles of varying difficulty and piece count
- Small prizes

MAKE IT HAPPEN

- Set up the room with enough tables to have at least three puzzle stations of increasing difficulty. Decide on the rules for your challenge.
  - Will participants play individually or on teams?
  - Will there be different age and experience categories?
  - Will each round let all players complete the puzzle and rank their times, or will everyone race the clock and be ranked on how complete their puzzles are at the buzzer?
- The first round will begin with easier puzzles and progress to more difficult ones.
- Set your timers, put on some competitive music ("Eye of the Tiger," anyone?), and have some fun!

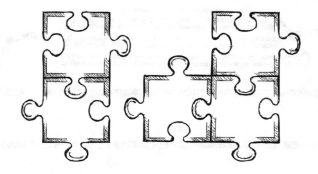

Green Teens

Teens are more environmentally conscious than any generation before them, and with good reason. Resources are dwindling, and garbage is clogging up land. This club will engage teens' community spirit while showing fun, creative ways to help the environment.

POWER PROMOTION

- Put information about upcoming Green Teens meetings right on recycling containers throughout the library to advertise to the target market.
- Re-use old flyers by printing the information for Green Teens on the back. Teens can help draw an X through the old side and will likely appreciate the re-use of the paper.

CROSSOVER PROGRAMS

- Big Paper Blooms—Crafting for Charity
- Geocaching—Scientific Teens
- Library Garden—Active Teens
- Promoting Yourself—Newsworthy Teens
- Trashion Show—Fashionista Teens

▣ Recycling Challenge

Make recycling unusual items a drive or challenge for the community. Many times people do not know where to take items such as inkjet printer cartridges or small electronics, and the library could partner with the city or village to collect those items. The teens could be responsible for promoting the event, counting donations, and possibly even bringing the items to the local recycling center.

SHOPPING LIST

- Nothing needs to be purchased for this program, but plan ahead and save or collect large boxes to be used as collection containers.
- If adding a competitive element, purchase small prizes (see Variations).

MAKE IT HAPPEN

- Contact local waste or recycling centers to determine how inkjet printer cartridges or electronics can be recycled.
- Invite teens to help cover and decorate large boxes for collection.
- Define parameters of the challenge. Will electronics be collected during Teen Tech Week? Is the end of the school year a good time to obtain inkjet cartridges as teens print papers? Let teens in the club choose what should be collected and for how long. Teens should also set a goal to make this event a challenge, or they can just post how many have been collected to keep promoting the event.

VARIATIONS

- Complete a List of Recycling Activities to Get a Prize: Patrons who complete a list of recycling activities could get a prize such as a packet of seeds or mini recycled notebooks. Activities can include donating to the teen drive, bringing materials to a local thrift store or donation center, donating items to the Flea Market (another Green Teens program), making mulch, and more.

ONLINE

- A Green Teens site on the library page could indicate what is being collected and where in the community for easy drop-off.

➡ Garden Art

Teens can make and decorate garden stakes for art or for use in gardens at this session. They may opt to sell these at a Flea Market event as well.

SHOPPING LIST

- Table coverings
- 18- to 24-inch-long wooden dowel rods or PVC pipes for stakes, at least ¾ to 1 inch wide
- Outdoor epoxy glue
- Small watering cans, small seasonal figures, or other flat-bottomed items that can be glued on top of the stakes. (Teens should check their garages and basements at home, or staff may find objects at thrift stores.)

MAKE IT HAPPEN

- Find a space where stakes may be inverted and stored undisturbed for a couple of days until dry for this project.
- Show teens gardening magazines for inspiration.
- Instruct teens on how to secure objects with glue to dowel rods or pipes. Projects may need to be inverted to dry.

VARIATIONS

- Garden Art Tour: Teens can invite people to take pictures of unusual or creative garden art around the community and post for inspiration, or teens can post their own.

ONLINE

- Virtual Garden Scavenger Hunt: After the club makes the stakes, ask for permission to keep and photograph them during the summer at other teen-friendly locations. Invite teens to guess where those locations are from photos of the stake (with some background so they can figure it out). This event will further promote the Green Teens.

RESOURCES

15-Minute Garden Projects: www.midwestliving.com/garden/ideas/15-minute-garden -projects/page/0/0

Easy Fall Pumpkin Garden Stakes: www.birdsandbloomsblog.com/2013/09/21/easy-fall -pumpkin-garden-stakes

⮕ Flea Market

Green Teens can host a flea market event or flea market table at the library to recycle materials. Teens can sell used items, create items to sell from craft materials to raise money, or coordinate an event for adults and teens to sell things.

SHOPPING LIST

- Price tags (painter's tape also works) and markers for pricing
- Money box (for collecting monies raised)
- Bags, boxes (donated)

MAKE IT HAPPEN

- Have teens define parameters, including what ages will be allowed to host tables and shop, whether there will be a fee for table registration, where the fees will go (toward library or environmental causes), whether crafts will be allowed, and how long the event will run on what day.
- Teens will need to help advertise for table hosts and shoppers well before the event. Table hosts should register by one month prior to the event with fees paid.
- The Green Teens could work with other teen clubs to make and sell objects at the event.
- One week before the event, send each registered table host a letter code. Hosts must price all materials with the letter code (for example, "A $1"). These will be used to ring up sales.
- When shoppers select items, one teen will write down all codes and costs, another will take money and make change, and others will help pack using the donated bags and boxes.
- At the end of the event, teens will total and return monies to hosts depending on sales.

VARIATIONS

- All-Donation Flea Market: The flea market can consist of donated items or books, and all collected monies can go to the library programs. Staff can help teens determine the value of materials.
- Flea Market Table: Teens can maintain a swap table in the library on particular days where people bring and take reading, listening, or viewing materials.

→ Rain Barrel Decoration

Rain barrels are a great way to cut down on water use and waste. In this program, teens decorate rain barrels for their homes, for the library, or for a local charity auction.

CROSSOVER

- Crafting for Charity

SHOPPING LIST

- Rain barrels (many kinds can be found at home improvement stores and can store up to 200 gallons; large, white plastic ones are good for decorating)
- Light sandpaper (to prepare the surface of a washed rain barrel)
- High-quality primer paint (rain barrel will require 3 to 4 coats)
- Acrylic paints (for decorating)
- Polyurethane (for a finishing coat)
- Paintbrushes
- Paper towels *or* disposable shop rags (for cleanup)

MAKE IT HAPPEN

- One week before: The rain barrels must be prepared in a few steps throughout the week before the program, either by teens or staff. Wash and lightly sand the rain barrels. Apply a few coats of primer and allow to dry.
- At the event: Show teens photos of decorated rain barrels found online. Invite teens to develop a theme for decoration. Even splatter paint or a sky with planets can be fun; the theme does not have to be just about plants and gardens.
- After the decoration is thoroughly dry, have teens apply two coats of polyurethane over the decoration on the outside of the barrels. It is best to do this outdoors because of fumes.

ONLINE

- Post photos of the rain barrels online and take online auction bids for a local charity.

RESOURCES

The Garden Diaries—Rain Barrel Eye Candy (start-to-finish rain barrel decoration): https://thegardendiaries.wordpress.com/2012/01/30/rain-barrel-eye-candy

▣ Forcing Potted Bulbs

This is a simple, hands-on project that helps deliver a bit of color in late winter and will give your Green Teens a way to get their hands dirty before the first thaw. Try layering the bulbs to give an extra blooming season. Force the bulbs by exposing the whole potted creation to cold before bringing it inside and enjoying beautiful blooms, even before spring's first crocuses pop up. Green Teens and budget-conscious libraries may take this on as a longer-term project by obtaining free bulbs from municipal organizations or shopping malls as they prepare for the next season's landscaping.

CROSSOVER

- Crafting for Charity

SHOPPING LIST

- Terra-cotta or recycled plastic pots
- Potting soil
- Gravel
- Scoops (can be plastic cups or trowels)
- Hearty spring bulbs like daffodils, crocus, and tulips
- Ribbons, permanent markers, and other embellishments for the pots
- Cards with instructions
- Table covers if the program is inside

MAKE IT HAPPEN

- Prepare your space:
  - If the program is inside, cover tables and consider putting down drop cloths.
  - Open bags of soil and gravel and provide a scoop for each bag.
  - Set out decorating supplies.
- Have teens decorate the pots.
- Instruct teens on how to plant the bulbs.
  - Place a layer of gravel in each pot to aid in drainage.
  - Fill the bottom of the pots with several inches of potting soil.
  - Plant a layer of bulbs, making sure that they are planted right side up (check the packaging) and do not touch one another.
  - Gently sprinkle more soil in until the bulbs are covered.
  - Plant another layer of bulbs and cover them with soil as well.
- Teens can attach a card to each pot with easy-to-follow and easy-to-read instructions before delivering to their location of choice.

VARIATIONS

- Forcing the bulbs will provide spring blooms in the wintertime. But the project can also work as a springtime or Mother's Day gift and be displayed outside.
- For many people who have moved into assisted-living facilities or have limited ability to navigate their own homes and yards, the loss of their garden stings. Pair this activity with the Crafting for Charity Club to deliver winter blooms to shut-ins and nursing-home residents.

RESOURCES

Old House Gardens—Bulbs in Pots: www.oldhousegardens.com/BulbsInPots.aspx

This Old House—"Sandwich" Bulbs for Six Weeks of Blooms: www.thisoldhouse.com/toh/photos/0,,20295299,00.html

Weekend Gardener—Double Plant Bulbs: www.weekendgardener.net/flower-bulbs/double-planting-110911.htm

→ Working Worms: Vermicomposting Bins

For teens who really want to get up close with ecology- and earth-friendly practices, composting is a great habit to acquire. Vermicomposting takes the basic compost pile to a new level by adding specific varieties of worms to the compost bin, which will improve the quality and nutrient content of the compost. Better still, vermicomposting bins do not have an unpleasant odor and can be kept inside the home.

CROSSOVER

- Crafting for Charity
- Scientific Teens

SHOPPING LIST

- Two stacking 5- or 10-gallon plastic bins and 1 lid for each teen
- Red composting worms (see Resources), at least 1 pound per bin
- Roll of window screening (donated or purchased from a hardware store or a building materials surplus store)
- Drill with ¼-inch drill bit
- Dried leaves or grass clippings without pesticide residue
- Produce scraps
- Brown paper bags or other paper to shred
- Scissors

MAKE IT HAPPEN

- Guest Speakers: Contact local organic gardening groups, garden centers, university extension services, or vermicomposting clubs to invite experts to talk about how to successfully vermicompost. An added benefit is that you may find folks with worms to share, which would significantly reduce the cost of the program.
- Have teens watch Matthew Ross's TED-Ed talk, "Vermicomposting: How Worms Can Reduce Our Waste" (http://ed.ted.com/lessons/vermicomposting-how -worms-can-reduce-our-waste-matthew-ross), and have a conversation with teens about the benefits of vermicomposting.
- Instruct teens on how to make and maintain the bin.
  - Use the drill to punch holes in one of the bins: around the top perimeter spaced about 2 inches apart for air circulation and in a loose pattern on the bottom of the bin for drainage.

— Cut the window screen to fit in the bottom of the bin, covering the holes.

— Place the bin with the holes into the other bin without holes.

— Shred or rip into pieces the brown bag and other paper and use it to fill the bottom of the bin about three-quarters full.

— Pour water into the bin to soak the paper, then wring it out so that it is damp but not soaking wet. Drain off excess water and then fluff the paper with your hands.

— Add the worms and leave them alone to adjust to their new home. Teens take the bins home at this point.

— In a few days, add some compost material, ideally fluffing the paper and spreading the new material under the paper: use coffee grounds, produce scraps, and bread or other starchy scraps, but avoid fats, meats, and dairy products.

— Keep the vermicomposting bin damp but not wet. Drain the bin by removing the top bin from the bottom bin and dumping any excess water.

VARIATIONS

- If the cost is prohibitive for each teen to create a bin, consider creating one or two larger bins to be used in community locations: a school, a community garden, a park district building, or even the library!

- Partner with Active Teens to install a vermicomposting station in conjunction with their Library Garden program.

RESOURCES

Matthew Ross's TED-Ed Talk: http://ed.ted.com/lessons/vermicomposting-how-worms-can -reduce-our-waste-matthew-ross

Red Worm Composting: www.redwormcomposting.com

Wisconsin DNR—Environmental Education for Kids! Composting with Worms: http://dnr.wi .gov/org/caer/ce/eek/earth/recycle/compost2.htm

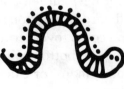
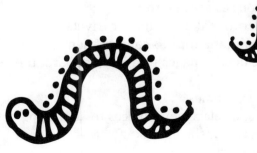

⮕ Reuse-Remake-Renew

Not enough is made of the second *R* in the "Reduce, Reuse, Recycle" mantra. This program aims to change that by giving old objects a second life. Consider scheduling this after your Recycling Challenge as a way to collect plenty of materials or as a part of a bigger promotional event.

CROSSOVER

- Crafting for Charity
- Fantastic Readers—Read-a-Latte Books and Media Club
- Out of This World—Read-a-Latte Books and Media Club
- Technology Makers

SHOPPING LIST

- All of the supplies for this event can–and ideally should—be recyclables. Consider sourcing items from Freecycle if your community has a group.
- Pull out any half-used rolls of duct tape, leftover craft supplies, paint bottles with just a few dabs left. Invite teens to bring items in from home that they're no longer using, either for their own project or for someone else to draw on for inspiration. Open wide the doors of that craft cabinet and see just how creative your teens can be!
- Teens will benefit from having Internet access or craft books and magazines for this program.

MAKE IT HAPPEN

- Make sure all of your recycled supplies are clean.
- Show teens some examples of reusing objects to give them a second, useful life. Pinterest is a great place to find these ideas. Here are some examples:
  - Knit or crochet plastic grocery bags into floor mats.
  - Poke small holes in the bottoms of milk jugs to provide a slow watering method for new garden plantings.
  - Use cardboard egg cartons as seed starters.
  - Glue wine corks together to make coasters or trivets.
  - Sew closed the bottoms of tank tops to convert them into tote bags.
  - Glue photos, maps, or calendar pages to thin cardboard, then cut them apart into puzzles.
  - Wind yarn around picture frames.
  - Use old hardware, gears, or electronics pieces to adorn goggles, necklaces, or picture frames and create a steampunk effect.
  - Do any number of art projects!

- Have teens browse the Internet or books and magazines for ideas based on the recyclables that have been collected and the supplies that are available—and get to work!

VARIATIONS

- Display the items teens create as a way to encourage attendance at the club and to demonstrate to library visitors all the ways they can reuse their own items instead of contributing to landfills.
- Do this project before a Friends of the Library book sale and add teens' creations to the sale as a fund-raiser for club activities.

RESOURCES

Freecycle allows people to freely request, offer, and receive items that would otherwise be destined for the landfill: www.freecycle.org

Pinterest.com

Newsworthy Teens

This club incorporates writing skills, photography, social media, and trends as teens find news about themselves and others and bring it to the world. It may be fun to start this club over the summer with teens who want to work on a library site or newspaper, and build it from there. Teens will see how news and news reporting change the world.

POWER PROMOTION

- As teens write their own news bulletins through library and their own sites, word of the club will spread.
- At one of the first meetings, talk to teens about how to publicize the group and develop a consistent credit line or two that they can attach to pieces they write.
- Local papers may allow teens to submit clips or public relations articles about teen events or photographs from library events. Information can be included about the Newsworthy Teens Club in those works.

CROSSOVER PROGRAMS

- Just One Sentence Journaling—Scrapbooking and Photography
- Read-a-Latte Books and Media Club
- Taking the Fear Out of Public Speaking—Entertaining Teens
- Phone Photography or Movie Contest—Scrapbooking and Photography

➡ Promoting Yourself

How teens present themselves makes an impact on their news reporting—and news making—opportunities. Informal and formal gatherings and online presence tips will be covered. This meeting can pair with Taking the Fear Out of Public Speaking, an Entertaining Teens session.

CROSSOVER

- Entertaining Teens

SHOPPING LIST

- Nothing needs to be purchased for this session. You may want to provide pens and paper, a laptop and projector, and fun props such as a tie or jacket.

MAKE IT HAPPEN

Informal and Networking Interactions: Talk to teens about how the impression made at an informal gathering can be instant and distorted. When teens arrive, ask them to shake hands and introduce themselves to each other. After a few minutes, ask teens to discuss who made a great impression on them and why. (Don't ask about negatives!) Discuss as a group how to make a good impression with eye contact, handshakes, and polite but energetic conversation and demeanor. How could they successfully ask someone for a quote for an article? Teens may also want to talk about situations where networking can be important.

Formal Meetings: Invite teens to provide bad examples of a news interview acting as either the interviewer or interviewee. You may want to film these. After each, have teens discuss what went wrong and why.

Phone Interview: Teens are not always familiar with phone etiquette in a world where they usually text. Again, ask for bad examples and then good ones and discuss.

E-mail: Ask teens how often they share or forward text messages or Facebook posts. Then discuss e-mail etiquette and how to pitch someone for an interview or story. What kinds of questions should be asked? What is an appropriate length for an e-mail message?

Other Social Media: Discuss the difference between how teens might use social media to communicate with one another and how media outlets and celebrities use social media to promote themselves. How are the language and grammar different? What about the platforms used and the frequency of posting? Have teens find media outlets using social media in ways that they connect to, and those that they think could be improved.

ONLINE —————————————————————————————————

- Worst News Interview Video Clips Contest: Invite teens to submit video clips of bad news interview skits and post entries.
- News Reporter Fashion Show: Post possible outfits for various news gathering occasions (ask teens to bring in different looks and model them) and have voting and discussion.

TWEET
SOCIAL MEDIA
CHAT
NETWORK
E-MAIL
BLOG

➡ Cartoon Capers

Teens will learn about the history of cartooning and the effectiveness of cartoon messages versus entertainment styles. They can also try some techniques.

CROSSOVER

- Anime and Manga Readers and Viewers— Read-a-Latte Books and Media Club

SHOPPING LIST

- Nothing needs to be purchased for this session. Provide pencils and blank paper so teens can try cartooning techniques. You may wish to project some cartoons or show short clips of cartoons.

MAKE IT HAPPEN

- Famous Characters: Choose some famous characters and pull information about the history of those characters along with samples. Examples include Snoopy, Blondie, Calvin and Hobbes, Dilbert, or the Simpsons. Ask teens to identify themes and style aspects as well as discuss why some cartoons are popular at different times.
- Political versus Strip Cartoons: Show samples of political cartoons from newspapers or the *New Yorker* and have teens identify why a single panel can be more effective than an article.
- Comic Books: Show teens several samples of superhero comics and graphic novels and discuss their appeal. Do teens like story arcs and having to wait for the next issue?
- Children's Cartoon Books: Discuss why children love the Wimpy Kid, Captain Underpants, and Bone series, or other titles the teens may remember.
- Television or Movie Cartoons: Show some clips from holiday or serial cartoons and ask who they believe watches these and why.
- Drawing: Invite teens to try drawing and writing a single-panel cartoon depicting something unfair in their lives.

ONLINE

- An online poll or discussion of favorite characters or cartoon books is one way to engage teens on this topic.
- Cartoon Contest: Offer prizes to teens for depicting a news event in single-panel cartoon form.

➲ Photo and Video Blogs

Blogging is taking new forms online as different social media platforms become popular, but the basic skills remain. In this program, teens will go over making interesting yet appropriate posts, building an audience, and using interactive elements of blogs.

CROSSOVER

- Entertaining Teens

SHOPPING LIST

- Teens will need access to computers and cameras for this session.

MAKE IT HAPPEN

- Set up accounts for basic blogs at Blogger and WordPress for library use. Also set up Vine, Instagram, Tumblr, and Twitter feeds (or whichever media are popular with the teens attending) so teens may experiment with those if they are unfamiliar with them.
- Ask teens to discuss or find some blogs that interest them. What makes those blogs unique? Pull up some of author John Green's video posts (www.youtube .com/user/vlogbrothers) or other popular blogs. Are there blogs on a particular topic such as Minecraft that are especially appealing to the teens?
- Have teens talk about why some blogs are not interesting. Go over how consistency in posting, variety, and various visual or video formats enhance blogs. Discuss what too much personal information to post is.
- Have teens make up subjects for five blog posts. Go over how to do simple posting with a picture on Blogger or WordPress.
- Show teens how to schedule posts ahead of time.
- Instruct teens on how to share posts on different social media, such as Facebook or Twitter.
- Split the group into smaller clusters to make video posts with phones or microphones and computers. Post them on the sample blogs.

ONLINE

- Ask for teen guest bloggers for the library site. Schedule one or two a week. If participation is low, invite book reviews, either in print or video, as part of a reading promotion and post those.
- Post trivia or have another teen contest as part of the blog and invite the club to come up with topics and questions.
- Make a section of links to favorite teen blogs as well as blogs by teen club members.

⮕ Interview Skills

Giving, conducting, and taking notes on a good interview are critical skills for teens interested in the news. Interviewing is also a straightforward way to get comfortable in front of and behind the camera. This program gives teens a structured setting in which to test out and improve their skills. Later, they can use these skills as they seek out and report news in or outside the library.

CROSSOVER

- Entertaining Teens

SHOPPING LIST

- Camera (either stand-alone or on a phone)
- Projector (for evaluating the interviews)

MAKE IT HAPPEN

- Set up the camera and projector in a quiet location.
- Have a conversation with teens about what they think makes a good interview. Talk about things like the following:
  - Subject matter
  - Interviewer's approach
  - Types of questions
  - How to put the subject at ease
- Watch some interviews on YouTube and talk about which ones were good, which were bad, and why.
- Break the group into teams of three: cameraperson, interviewer, and subject. Each team should find a place to set up an interview, decide on a topic, and conduct a brief interview—three minutes or so. For this practice interview, encourage the teams to choose topics that the teens being interviewed are comfortable with and knowledgeable about: favorite movies, how their favorite sports teams are doing, or some hot gossip from school this week.
- Have teens swap roles and conduct another interview until each teen gets a turn in each role.
- Show each interview and talk about what worked, what didn't work, and what teens might do differently next time.

VARIATIONS

- For more sophisticated teens, consider playing with different settings and lighting options and external microphones to decide what works best.
- Once teens have the interviews, let them try their writing or podcasting skills by turning the interviews into fodder for an article or story.

RESOURCES

Katie Couric on how to conduct a good interview: www.youtube.com/watch?v = 4eOynrI2eTM

➡ The Medium and the Message

News comes to us now in more ways than ever. How do you know which method is the best for getting your message across? This conversation-style program encourages teens to think critically about how they get their news and what the best venue is for sharing their own news.

SHOPPING LIST

- Computers with Internet access

MAKE IT HAPPEN

- With teens, brainstorm all the various ways they or people they know acquire news. Newspapers, radio, TV, websites, magazines, Facebook sharing, Twitter, podcasts, Vine, and more all may come up.
- Ask which ones teens prefer. Which do they avoid?
- Discuss whether there are types of news that seem particularly suited to particular mediums. How do teens prefer to learn about sports news as opposed to social activism? Where do they go to learn about celebrities as opposed to major national news? Is one form of news broadcasting *better* than another?
- Consider a recent news event. Encourage teens to locate as many stories in different mediums as possible.
- Have teens compare the way the reporting looks, sounds, and feels from the newspaper to the TV report to a blog post to the Twitter feed. Which serves the story best? Which seems the most authoritative? Which seems the most current? Which do they trust the most?
- Encourage teens to take what they've learned into practice as they write news pieces for their blogs, library sources, and the like.

VARIATIONS

- Take the plot of a popular book or movie and have teens report on it in a variety of formats. How would they talk about it differently in a major newspaper rather than on a blog?

⏩ A Picture's Worth . . .

We all know what a picture's worth. But how to make it worth even more? Get it to tell a really compelling story. This program walks teens through several different types of photography that might be used to tell a story, then gives them a chance to test their eye.

CROSSOVER

- Scrapbooking and Photography

SHOPPING LIST

- Cameras
- Computers

MAKE IT HAPPEN

- Pull newspapers, books, and websites to illustrate the different types of photography that teens will encounter in news making. Find examples of the following:
  - Features
  - Commercial
  - Travel
  - Sports
  - Human interest
  - Environmental/Scene Setting
- Talk about why a journalist would use one type of photograph instead of another. Show some of the examples you've pulled and talk about what works and what doesn't.
- Send teens out into the library, the neighborhood, or a program to take some photos that they think tell the story of the event or scene that they are trying to capture. Give teens fifteen minutes or less—pretend this is breaking news!
- When they return to the program room, have teens swap their cameras with one another. Now they are the "editors" and will choose the photograph—taken by someone else—that they think best describes the event.
- Have the photographer and the editor talk about why they made the selection and whether those are the pictures that the photographer would choose.

VARIATIONS

- Prearrange this event to coincide with a big library program so that teens have a subject at the ready and the library has lots of photos after the fact.
- Give pairs of teens different types of photos to capture. Teens can have fun trying to re-create a sports photo or imagining or re-creating a scene complete with characters (a candidate who has just lost an election, a family greeting a soldier who has come home from abroad, the winning volleyball team accepting their trophies, an author learning of an award won or lost) to photograph and try to capture the mood.

RESOURCES

Mike Davis—What Is a Newspaper Photograph? www.michaelddavis.com/blog/2011/2/8/ what-is-a-newspaper-photograph.html

⇨ Deadline!

There's no procrastinating in a newsroom. Every second counts. This program gives teens a chance to test their journalistic grace under pressure. Partnering with Entertaining Teens would give the entertainers a chance to stage a scene—crime or otherwise—for the newshounds to report on. If that's not possible, showing an online clip will give teens enough to go on to write their stories. Ready, set, GO!

CROSSOVER

- Entertaining Teens

SHOPPING LIST

- Notebooks and pens
- Computers
- Projector (will work best if you opt to show a video scene for teens to report on)

MAKE IT HAPPEN

- Set up the projector or stage and give each teen a notebook.
- Explain that you are the editor, sending them out to report on a crime or event already in progress, but don't give them many more details to go on. As the busy editor, you've gotta get back to work already!
- Cue the actors or turn on the video clip (see Resources).
- If working with teen actors, give them a chance to practice their improv skills by allowing the reporters to question them for quotes or more information.
- After the scene concludes, tell the teens how many column inches (one column inch is between thirty and forty words) are available for their stories and how soon you will need them.
- Set the timer and encourage teens to get to work!
- At the end of the allotted time, invite teens to read their articles aloud. Compare and contrast their work. Hold an informal vote to select the teen whose article best captures the scene.

ONLINE

- In conjunction with The Medium and the Message, have teens write the story in different ways to fit their chosen medium: traditional daily paper, local interest newspaper, Twitter, news blog, vlog, or online magazine.

RESOURCES

Livestreaming video, whether it's actually live or has been uploaded from a previous event, can give teens a person-on-the-street view of events. An overabundance of videos—from car crashes to award ceremonies to scientific breakthroughs to "stupid human tricks"—are freely available on YouTube and would work well for this challenge. You can also browse through the following sites to locate a clip or livestream that can provide teens with source material for Project Deadline!

Livestream: http://new.livestream.com
Ustream: www.ustream.tv

Scientific Teens

Showing how fun and relevant science can be may encourage some teens toward rewarding careers. The popularity of forensics shows may also heighten interest in crime-solving science and other applications. This club will show science in action through interactive projects.

POWER PROMOTION

- Advertise handwriting analysis and forensics subjects with a small crime scene in the teen area of the library.
- A shelf with books knocked down, a wrinkled but still visible note, crime scene tape, and assorted items such as a pen or a glove can catch teens' eyes.
- On a flyer advertising the club, invite teens to solve the crime and to bring their deduction to the meeting.
- Posters or displays could have mysterious objects in jars or bubbling liquids (easier on a poster).

CROSSOVER PROGRAMS

- Baking Basics—Food Fans
- Chocolate Chip Cookie Science—Food Fans
- Out of This World—Read-a-Latte Books and Media Club

⮕ Paranormal Science?

Breakthroughs in science are often made by having a mind open to possibilities. Although study of the paranormal may not be as scientific to some as the study of medicine, it is a popular topic. With the proliferation of ghost hunting shows on television, teens may be curious about equipment and investigation of paranormal phenomena.

SHOPPING LIST

- Digital tape and video recorders
- Paper and pencils for surveys

MAKE IT HAPPEN

- Leave a digital recorder going for a few hours at night when the library is closed. Also tape with a video recorder. The area chosen should be a corner with possible mysterious noises, such as in a basement, and should not be drafty.
- Guest Speakers: Consider inviting members of a local ghost investigative unit (search online for "ghost hunting investigations [state, city]") to speak with teens about experiences and about how they got into their hobby. Another guest speaker might be a local antiques dealer, who may provide insights about superstitious objects such as Ouija boards and legends associated with them.
- Invite teens to view and listen to the recordings from the library to see if they detect any "evidence." Show some video clips from ghost hunting television shows or clips amateurs have gathered and ask teens to discuss whether the clips are real and why they feel that way.
- Research local folklore and tell teens about any possible hauntings in the area. Show them articles and accounts of what was found there.

ONLINE

- Map of local history: Put a map of the local area online with links to information about possible paranormal incidents and ask for input on experiences.
- Survey of shows and beliefs: In an anonymous survey, ask teens how they feel about ghost hunting shows and the possibility of haunting.

→ Forensic Fun

Although law enforcement and forensic expert speakers are usually a draw for teens, you can do many CSI-type activities to show teens some of the science involved. This program invites teens to try some simple, interactive evidence-collecting techniques.

SHOPPING LIST

- Paper and pens

For the Blood Spatter Analysis
- Cornstarch
- Corn syrup
- Food coloring (red and green)
- Sponges
- Large sheets of paper
- Hammer, bat, or other blunt objects

For the Crime Scene Photographs
- Props to simulate a crime scene
- Cameras

MAKE IT HAPPEN

Guest Speakers: Invite local law enforcement officials or forensic teachers to discuss trends and tools in this specialized science.

Handwriting Analysis: Invite teens to discuss how and when handwriting analysis is used in modern times and why handwriting analysis is important. When can signatures be forged? Have everyone write the same sentence. First, have teens use the handwriting analysis sites listed in the Resources section to discover some personality traits that may be conveyed by the handwriting samples. Then ask teens to pass the paper to their left and try to forge the handwriting. Have them pass the paper again and identify where the first and second samples differ.

Blood Spatter Analysis: Reeko's Mad Scientist Lab, a science site for kids, outlines a messy but educational way to make fake blood with food coloring and cornstarch, then apply it to a sponge and splatter it onto paper for analysis (http://reekoscience .com/Experiments/blood_splatter_spatter_analysis.aspx#.Ukc5FpGDet8). The site also provides images of spatters and resulting deductions if it's not feasible to do the experiment during a club session.

DNA Collection: Ask teens where they might find DNA samples in the library (but don't do it—yuck!). Ask them to discuss whether all crimes can be solved by DNA. Discuss the CSI courtroom effect whereby juries believe DNA samples can be discovered within minutes and can solve every crime and ask whether teens think this will be the case in the future.

Photography: Ask teens to take photos of a concocted crime scene made of props at the library. If a house is robbed, what photos should be taken? How could a photograph be misleading? Teens should compare their photographs and show that different angles can change interpretation.

Witnesses: Ask one teen to leave the room. Before she returns, ask everyone else to detail what she was wearing. How reliable is witness testimony? What should teens look at or take note of if something is happening in their vicinity?

VARIATIONS

- Any one of the activities could be the focus of one club session, and this topic could be stretched to more than one meeting. For example, to continue the eyewitness testimony discussion, have an actor run into the room, steal an object, and run out again. Then ask teens to write down what happened. They could also go out in the parking lot and have five seconds to describe the first car they see.

ONLINE

- Post photos taken from different angles of a contrived crime scene at the library along with a form for teens to identify what happened and why. Prizes can be given for the most creative answer and the most logical answer.

RESOURCES

Forensic Science Lesson Plan Links: http://sciencespot.net/Pages/classforscilsn.html
How Handwriting Analysis Works: http://science.howstuffworks.com/handwriting-analysis1.htm
What Does Your Handwriting Say about You? http://visual.ly/what-does-your-handwriting-say-about-you

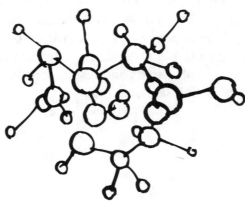

⮕ Time Travel Trivia

Technology predicted in past science fiction has come true in some cases. This trivia game can be designed by teens or prepared ahead by you and just played by them with either text or photos.

CROSSOVER

- Out of This World: Read-a-Latte Books and Media Club

SHOPPING LIST

- Prizes (classic science fiction paperbacks, temporary tattoos, or other small giveaways)

MAKE IT HAPPEN

- Pull classic science fiction books or movies, such as titles by Jules Verne, George Orwell, and Isaac Asimov. Pull some steampunk and current science fiction titles. Ask teens to identify paragraphs describing futuristic practices or technology.
- Also pull images from past and current media. Magazines on medicine, transportation, technology, and science are best, though articles on "futuristic" household helpers would also work. This is also a good way to show teens how to search online magazine databases to which the library subscribes.
- Put text or images describing technology, machinery, medicine, or robotics on paper or on a website and ask teens which are fictional and which are real.

VARIATIONS

- Although teens will enjoy putting this together, staff may do so and have all teens play.

⮕ Geocaching

Geocaching has been described as real-life treasure hunting. This is a fun, active way to engage teens with the world around them, with GPS use, and with mapping and compass use. What's more, it's a hobby that they can take just about anywhere in the world. A geocache, or cache, is a small container that is hidden, usually outside. The person who hides the cache then logs its location on a website (see Resources), sometimes with a hint or clue related to the location. Then, geocachers, people wanting to find a cache, obtain the coordinates of the desired cache online and head outdoors to try to find it.

CROSSOVER

- Active Teens
- Green Teens
- Traveling Teens

SHOPPING LIST

- To find caches, teens will need either a GPS, a GPS app on a smartphone, or a detailed topographic map and compass. All afford different learning opportunities.
- If your group wants to plant and maintain a cache of their own, you will need:
  - A small, waterproof container
  - A small notebook and golf pencil (to place in the container)
  - A few small items that fit into the container (plastic toys, interesting foreign coins, giveaways from past library promotions, etc.)

MAKE IT HAPPEN

- Create a free account on Geocaching.com.
- Use the search feature to find some caches that are near the library. Caches can be found all over the world, and you might be surprised by how many of these hidden treasures are already in your neighborhood. If you can't find one within a reasonable distance of the library for the purposes of this program, take up the challenge and plant one yourself!
- Talk to teens about what geocaching is and how to be a good steward of the game.
  - Be respectful of the land where you are hunting for the cache.
  - When you find it, log your visit in the notebook and exchange a small token of your own for something in the cache.
  - Return the cache to its location so others will be able to find it.
  - When you log your find online, don't give away its location by solving any hints or clues.

- Talk about GPS use and how to decipher coordinates.
- Alternately, locate topographic maps of the area and talk about compass use.
- Encourage teens to get outside and have some fun!

VARIATIONS

- Plant a cache with a series of library- or science-related clues and log its location online.
- Green Teens will enjoy geocaching for the opportunity to get outside and clean up their community while seeking caches.
- Active Teens can use this as an opportunity to tackle some hiking near their homes.
- Traveling Teens will discover the secret curiosities of their own neighborhoods. They may also want to plant a cache to draw others to great spots not to be missed.

ONLINE

- Be sure to log your finds on the Geocaching site. Use social media to encourage other patrons to seek out the caches you've found or placed as well.

RESOURCES

Geocaching: www.geocaching.com
Geocaching without GPS: www.youtube.com/watch?v = BqRn0tZzEyw
How Teens Discover Geocaching: www.geocaching.com/blog/2011/07/teens-and-geocaching

➡ Spin-Off Challenge

For several years, NASA's Goddard Space Flight Center has offered a Spinoff Challenge to teens and youth. In this challenge, participants take an innovation developed by NASA for the space program and spin it off into a new purpose here on earth. If you have eager teens and want a project that will take several sessions, check out the Resources section for information on how to participate in this video challenge. For this pared-down version of the program, teens will work in teams in a competitive thought exercise that can be completed in one session.

CROSSOVER

- Technology Makers

SHOPPING LIST

- Notepads and pens *or* wipe-off boards or chalkboards *or* building materials like cardboard and duct tape, LEGOs, pipe cleaners, and craft supplies
- Internet access
- Flip or cell phone camera (optional)

MAKE IT HAPPEN

- Create a list of scientific innovations or accidental inventions. Draw on those put forth by NASA (see Resources) or pull from scientific news. Alternately, haul a few years' worth of *Popular Science* or other scientific magazines into your program room and let teens find the innovations themselves!
- Explain the challenge, using some examples of technology designed for one purpose but now being used for another.
- Have the teens form teams. The first challenge is to decide on an innovation that teens think they can repurpose into a new use.
- After the teams have decided on a technology, give them a time limit to create their spin-off. Encourage them to draw or construct a mock-up of their technology.
- Invite teens to rehearse or film a thirty-second ad for their product.
- Bring the group back together to share their ads. Talk about the technologies used and invented and vote on favorites.

ONLINE

- Use social media to spark interest in the challenge by sharing cool technologies and starting conversations about how they could be spun off.
- Share videos created by the teens and encourage the conversation to continue as the ideas really get cooking.

RESOURCES

Bridgman, Roger. *1,000 Inventions and Discoveries*. DK Publishing, 2014.
NASA Goddard Optimus Prime Spinoff Challenge: http://itpo.gsfc.nasa.gov/optimus
"NASA Spin-off Technologies": http://en.wikipedia.org/wiki/NASA_spin-off_technologies

⮕ Squishy Circuits

Teens learn the basics of electrical circuitry with playdough in this process developed by the Playful Learning Lab at the University of St. Thomas. "But," you say, "playdough is for little kids—these are *teens* we're talking about." Yes, they are teens who will love getting their hands back into this fun material from their childhood and using it in a whole new way. The electronic components for this project can be purchased online or at electronics stores for very little money and can be reused in future projects.

SHOPPING LIST

For the Circuits
- A Squishy Circuits kit (see Resources)
  or
- LEDs
- Small motors
- Wrapped copper wire
- 6V lantern battery
- Multimeter (optional)

For the Squishy
- Flour
- Salt
- Cream of tartar
- Sugar
- Vegetable oil
- Food coloring
- Deionized water

MAKE IT HAPPEN

Make two batches of playdough using the following recipes. The sugar dough can be made by the teens, but the salt dough requires stove-top prep and should be made ahead of time.

Salt (Conductive) Dough
- In a saucepan, stir to combine:
- 1 cup flour
- ¼ cup salt
- 3 tablespoons cream of tartar

Then add:
- 1 cup water
- 1 tablespoon vegetable oil
- food coloring

Cook over medium heat, stirring constantly. The mixture will get smooth, then get clumpy. Keep stirring until it forms a ball in the center of the pan. Remove from the pan onto a smooth surface with ½ cup flour. With caution, knead the hot dough into the flour until it is combined.

Sugar (Insulating) Dough
In a bowl, mix:
- 1½ cups flour
- ½ cup sugar
- 3 tablespoons vegetable oil
- ½ cup deionized water
- food coloring (use a different color than the conductive dough)
- Stir until combined and then knead until smooth.

Set up the supplies and give the teens the ground rules for safety and fun:
- One color dough is conductive—electricity will pass through it. The other is insulating—electricity will not pass through it.
- Don't touch the LED wires directly to the battery contacts.
- Don't connect the battery contacts to each other.

You can now either give them the instructions available at the Squishy Circuits page (see Resources) for building various types of circuits or just let them loose with the material. Letting teens explore the material and what it can do without so much direction may lead to more discovery.

VARIATIONS

- This is an ideal pairing for Technology Makers.
- Incorporate a MaKey MaKey into the squishy circuit play to turn the dough into controllers for computer games.
- Add small motors or buzzers to the LEDs for extra fun.
- Incorporate other craft and play materials to see what contraptions teens can come up with.

RESOURCES

Squishy Circuits: http://courseweb.stthomas.edu/apthomas/SquishyCircuits/index.htm

◈ Sharpie T Chromatography

Tie-dyed T-shirts are a perennial favorite with teens. This project simplifies the process into something that can be done with very little prep or cleanup. Additionally, teens can learn the basics of chromatography—separating colors into their component compounds— as they watch their Sharpie marks change with the help of simple household rubbing alcohol. If your teens are not interested in creating T-shirts but want to try their hands at chromatography by itself, the same process can be achieved by using coffee filters.

CROSSOVER

- Fashionista Teens

SHOPPING LIST

- Multicolored Sharpies *or* other permanent markers
- T-shirts (preferably white)
- Coffee filters
- Rubbing alcohol
- Spray bottle *or* eye droppers
- Large plastic cups
- Rubber bands
- Iron and ironing board

MAKE IT HAPPEN

- Work in a well-ventilated room or outside.
- Instruct teens on how to make the T-shirt.
  - Stretch the shirt over the mouth of the cup and fasten with a rubber band to create a taut circle or spread the coffee filter flat.
  - Using the Sharpies or markers, color on the circle in the desired pattern, understanding that once rubbing alcohol is applied, the ink will spread.
  - Repeat this until the shirt is covered as desired with colorful circles.
  - Spray rubbing alcohol on the shirt. Experiment with different methods— hanging the shirt and spraying top to bottom, leaving the shirt on the cups and spraying the center, or randomly spraying as desired.
  - The shirt will dry fairly quickly. Once dry, iron with the heat on the highest setting recommended to help set the ink.
- To examine the chromatography, have teens look at how individual colors separate. Ask the following questions: What color is black *really*? How do the colors change given more time to separate out? Do you find any surprises in the colors that emerge? How is this color exploration different than what you see when you mix paint? Or when you mix different colors of light? How would this be different if you used different types of markers?

RESOURCES

Sharpie to Tie-Dye For: http://blog.sharpie.com/2008/11/sharpie-to-tie-dye-for

Scrapbooking and Photography

Teens may want to document their lives in artistic styles that are more visually appealing than a social media page. A club that features scrapbooking and photography can feature a skill or project each month and just let teens work on current projects. Digital tools bring another aspect to these arts and may bring teens with different skills together to inspire each other.

POWER PROMOTION

- Clubs with beautiful, visual projects advertise themselves with online or physical displays.
- Invite teens to design their own publicity with creative photos, signs, or short videos from the club.

CROSSOVER PROGRAMS

- A Picture's Worth . . . —Newsworthy Teens
- Farewell Favorite Jeans!—Fashionista Teens
- Photo and Video Blogs—Newsworthy Teens

▣ Recipe Scrapbooking

With photos on their phones, teens may find it daunting to print pictures and make elaborate scrapbook pages for a themed album. Instead, this program provides a simple and appealing introduction to scrapbooking by showing teens how to gather some recipes for favorite foods.

CROSSOVER

- Food Fans

SHOPPING LIST

- 1-inch, three-ring binders (1 per teen)
- Plastic sheet protectors for binders (3–4 per teen)
- Scrapbooking paper in assorted colors and styles
- Die-cut food-themed shapes
- Food stickers
- Fancy-edged scissors (optional)
- Scissors
- Glue sticks
- Markers
- Copies of recipes (printed on one side of paper)

MAKE IT HAPPEN

- Teens may want to bring in their own favorite recipes for their scrapbook pages. Otherwise, make copies of several different recipes that they can cut and assemble into their pages.
- Teens can cut out recipes with fancy or straight-edged scissors, glue the recipes onto scrapbooking paper, and then decorate the pages with die-cuts or stickers.
- Instruct teens to put the pages in the sheet protectors and then in the binders.

VARIATIONS

- Have each teen bring in an ethnic family recipe and exchange copies before scrapbooking.
- Invite teens to gather recipes into one scrapbook for a charity auction event.
- Focus on themed recipes and decorations (for example, Scary Recipes for Halloween).

ONLINE

- Provide links to recipes with photos of scrapbook pages.
- Teens may want to try digital scrapbooking and can post their pages onto the website.

RESOURCES

Free Digital Scrapbooking: http://freedigitalscrapbooking.com

➡ Quilled Cards

The art of quilling has challenged crafters for hundreds and possibly thousands of years. Teens can try this craft and adapt it to three-dimensional cards and other projects for gifts.

CROSSOVER

- Crafting for Charity

SHOPPING LIST

- Quilling paper (⅜-inch and ⅛-inch strips are available through craft stores or can be made with thin origami paper)
- Quilling tools (toothpicks and fine, double-pointed knitting needles may be used)
- Gluing tool (glue sticks may be substituted for fine quilling glue tools)
- Plain cards
- Markers
- Scissors

MAKE IT HAPPEN

- Pull books or online information on basic quilling shapes. Briefly go over the history of quilling and show a tutorial so teens can see the process (or do a demonstration).
- Show teens how to wind strips around knitting needles to start. They may use finer needles as they get used to doing this. Have them glue the shapes onto the cards using glue sticks or glue tools.
- Encourage teens to decorate their cards with positive thinking-of-you or birthday messages for a local senior center or for friends.

VARIATIONS

- Quilled Jewelry: Teens who enjoy quilling may want to glue small shapes to fabric interfacing and attach them to earring hardware to make snowflakes, flowers, and more.
- Quilled Frames: Show teens how some quilled shapes can enhance a photo in a frame or on a scrapbooking page (use the ⅛-inch strips).

RESOURCES

North American Quilling Guild Official Shape Chart: www.naqg.org/accreditation/ NAQGshapeChartFinal2010.pdf
Quilling Basics—Shapes: www.quilledcreations.com/QuillingBasics-Shapes.asp

➡ Phone Photography or Movie Contest

Although anyone can snap a picture or take a short movie with a phone or iPad, skills are required to make a quality product. A phone photography contest can appeal to basic users, while a ten-second movie can inspire Vine and other short-movie aficionados.

CROSSOVER

- Newsworthy Teens

SHOPPING LIST

- Phones *or* iPads
- Prizes for winners in each category (iTunes gift certificates, etc.)

MAKE IT HAPPEN

- Three months before the contest begins, have Scrapbooking and Photography Club members volunteer to be judges for the contest and set the parameters of the contest. For example, teens can decide if the entire movie should be shot with sound or if editing will be allowed or required for the finished entries.
- To promote the event, club members may want to offer a session to help prospective contest entrants with shooting or editing. Teens can also film short commercials for the contest to be posted on websites and YouTube.
- At the end of the contest, have club members choose plenty of winners. Rather than first, second, and third per category, consider creative awards to include more teens (for example, funniest video, best pet photo, most mysterious photo, etc.).
- Teens can have a viewing night for photos and videos in place of a club meeting or as a special program.

VARIATIONS

- If teens are interested in video editing, categories for effects can be added and taught at library programs.

ONLINE

- This program can be done entirely online, ending with a photo and video gallery.
- Virtual Scavenger Hunt: Post a theme each week on library social media, such as favorite place to read, and draw winners from photos sent in.

⊡ Just One Sentence Journaling

Twitter and other social media feature brevity. Teens are used to this with texting. This program will highlight ways to write journal entries that are short if not sweet.

CROSSOVER

- Newsworthy Teens

SHOPPING LIST

- Teens can write entries electronically on laptops or phones, but paper and pens also work well for this program.

MAKE IT HAPPEN

- When teens come in, ask them to write down five things that recently happened to them.
- Ask them to rewrite each event in sentences of no more than one hundred words. This activity may be easier on a laptop that can quickly add word counts.
- Discuss what events should not be shortened, and ask teens to consider in what ways fewer words can be more powerful than a lengthy description. Invite them to rewrite one sentence with twice as many words and see which they like better. Pull some Twitter examples.
- Have teens try writing about major events in history in hundred-word sentences.
- Invite teens to write every day until the next meeting. They may link to a digital photo they take with entries if desired.

ONLINE

- This program can be done entirely online, emphasizing that personal information should not be shared in online forums.

→ Handmade Retro Photographs

Given the prevalence of artistic filters used to evoke a nostalgic tone, this program will be a hit with lots of teens. Using photographic colored pencils or paints, teens will turn black-and-white photographs into uniquely colored photos. They can go the traditional route and try to emulate hand-colored photos from the days before color photography was prevalent, or they can use the technique to play with color and turn run-of-the-mill photos into artistic masterpieces.

SHOPPING LIST

- Black-and-white photographs
- Photographic-quality colored pencils or paints (available at art supply shops)
- Books and examples of hand-colored photos

MAKE IT HAPPEN

- Show teens examples of hand-colored photos.
- Discuss why and how artists would hand-color photos instead of leaving them black and white. Talk about how the black-and-white versus color photos elicit different feelings and connections to the people and places.
- Examine photos that use hand tinting for realism as opposed to those that use hand tinting to accent specific features or to skew reality.
- Encourage teens to use the colored pencils or paints to creatively tint their photos.
- Discuss the results.

VARIATIONS

- This project can be done inexpensively on the fly by printing out black-and-white pictures on regular paper and using standard colored pencils for a similar effect.
- Encourage teens to give a modern photo a retro feel and vice versa through color choices.
- Compare the effects of hand-coloring photos to the effects produced by the automatic filters applied on Instagram and other photo-sharing sites.

RESOURCES

Hand Tint Photography: www.pinterest.com/mitchkd/hand-tint-photography
Hand-Tinted Photos and Other Early Colour Photographic Processes: www.pinterest.com/bird_museum/hand-tinted-photos-and-other-early-colour-photogra
Photo Coloring: www.dickblick.com/categories/photocoloring

→ Mini Photo Books

Way back before we carried hundreds of photos in our pockets by way of our cell phones, folks had little brag books tucked into purses and strips of photos in wallets. This mini photo book is a clever paper craft as well as a quaint way to display photos. It lends itself nicely to telling a photo essay and makes a nice gift or commemoration of an event.

CROSSOVER

- Crafting for Charity

SHOPPING LIST

- Colored paper card stock (acid-free preferable)
- Scissors
- Archive-quality glue sticks
- Photographs
- Markers, colored pencils
- Rulers
- Embellishments (ribbon, stickers, etc.)
- Folded paper book instructions (found online)

MAKE IT HAPPEN

- Provide a variety of folded paper book styles as examples. Allow teens to peruse them and decide on the best style for their purpose.
- Provide instructions (see Resources) for cutting and folding the photo books.
- Arrange the photos in the book to tell a story.
- Embellish the books with captions, quotes, and decorative accents.

RESOURCES

Minibook Gallery (with links to instructions): http://jimmielanley.hubpages.com/hub/minibooks-2#

→ Best. Trip. Ever. Scrapbook

Whether your teens are well traveled or only have great dreams of road trips and backpacking tours, this is a fun way to document or envision a great trip. Traveling Teens will likely have photographs of their journeys. For teens who haven't had many terrific adventures yet, pull out those donated *National Geographic* magazines and start them dreaming!

CROSSOVER

- Traveling Teens

SHOPPING LIST

- Photographs from trips
- Mementos (ticket stubs, postcards, etc.)
- Discarded travel magazines and guides
- Maps
- Embellishments
- Scrapbook pages
- Scissors
- Glue sticks
- Rulers
- Internet access and printer (for printing out other material to include)

MAKE IT HAPPEN

- Encourage teens to think about the story they want their travel scrapbook to tell. Is it a story about friendship? The changing landscape? A metaphoric personal journey? The path they want to take after graduation? A dream road trip hitting their favorite band's most famous haunts?
- Have them sketch out the plan for the story they decide on.
- Demonstrate ways to organize the images and mementos to tell their story.
- Encourage teens to include maps, embellishments, and journal entries to add details, hold on to memories, and add interest to the pages.

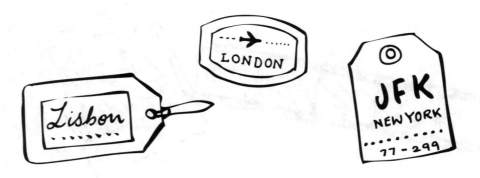

Technology Makers

Makerspace **is a** real buzzword these days. But you don't need to have a dedicated space to scratch the itch to create in a technical way, and even if you do have a dedicated maker area in your library, chances are the teens that gravitate there will appreciate an idea or two thrown their way now and then.

POWER PROMOTION

- Contact any local makerspaces in your area and talk up your club. Ask to leave flyers or business cards to hand to teens eager to do more.
- If your local schools have STEM clubs like the FIRST LEGO competition teams, advertise to them. Consider jumping onto any national or local STEM promotional events, such as the Imagination Foundation's Global Cardboard Challenge, NASA's Spinoff Challenge, or similar initiatives.
- In the library, stage a display with various pieces of equipment or a dismantled piece of electronics and a sign asking "What could you make with this?" and giving the information for the club's dates.

CROSSOVER PROGRAMS

- Intro to DJ Skills—Entertaining Teens
- Reuse–Remake–Renew—Green Teens
- Spin-Off Challenge—Scientific Teens
- Squishy Circuits—Scientific Teens

⮕ Touchscreen Gloves

This is a great program to ease teens into STEM and maker programs because it uses very traditional craft materials and techniques in a new way. Teens will use conductive thread to customize regular gloves into functional touchscreen capable gloves. Conductive thread is inexpensive and easily obtained at RadioShack or other similar electronics hobby stores.

SHOPPING LIST

- Conductive thread
- Sewing needles
- Inexpensive stretchy winter gloves
- Markers

MAKE IT HAPPEN

- Have the teens try on the gloves, then pretend that they are using a touchscreen device. This is to determine exactly where they want the conductive patch to be positioned.
- Have teens mark those spots with the marker, then insert the marker (cap on) into the finger or thumb of the glove. This is to prevent them from sewing the tip of the finger shut.
- Instruct teens on how to make the conductive patch.
  - Thread a needle with a few feet of conductive thread.
  - Using a simple satin stitch, sew back and forth over the marked spot until you have a large enough patch to make contact with the screen.
  - When you're done, insert the thread back into the pad you've created and cut it off, leaving a long enough tail inside the glove that the conductive thread is in good contact with your finger.
  - Repeat on the other desired fingers or thumbs.

RESOURCES

Review—Conductive Thread and DIY Touchscreen Gloves:

http://robottestkitchen.com/2014/11/13/review-conductive-thread-diy-touchscreen-gloves

Take Apart Tech

You could call this an UN-maker program, and it will absolutely thrill a certain set of teens—those who have been taking things apart since before they could talk, and those who have always been itching to give it a try. What makes a clock tick? What about a digital clock? What better way to find out than to take it all apart! Consider planning this event just before a local community electronics recycling event so that you can safely dispose of any items the teens play with.

SHOPPING LIST

- Inexpensive appliances (purchase at resale shops or ask coworkers to donate theirs instead of discarding them)
- Screwdrivers in a variety of sizes
- Allen wrenches in a variety of sizes

MAKE IT HAPPEN

- Before beginning, be warned that microwave ovens, televisions, and old computer monitors with CRTs (cathode ray tubes) should not be used for this event because they could have stored charges, which could be dangerous. If you're concerned, or if your teens really want to take apart a microwave oven, just ask for some help or advice from someone with more knowledge to guide you in how to safely discharge such items.
- Hand out the screwdrivers and wrenches and let teens have at it!
- If you'd like, after teens have taken their appliance completely apart, encourage them to put it back together again . . . and make it work.
- Better yet, see if they can combine the parts to make something new!

VARIATIONS

- You can turn this into a fix-it program—it may be more satisfying for teens to begin with a project that could very well work at the end.

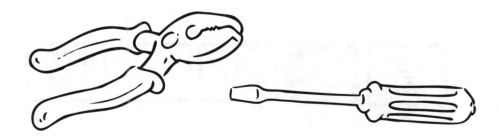

➡ Hour of Code

Each December, a week is designated to highlight the possibilities of learning computer coding. Your library can participate during this national week and reap the extra benefit of having nationwide promotion at your fingertips and being super current, or you could be a trailblazer and offer an Hour of Code any time of the year. The goal of this program is to highlight how rewarding it can be to learn some basic computer coding. Tutorials are freely available online, and the library can register as a location for an Hour of Code event. As the name implies, participants will spend just one hour coding, but will end up with some amazing results—and a certificate that proves they did it.

SHOPPING LIST

- Small prizes or rewards
- Internet-enabled computers

MAKE IT HAPPEN

- Because the program is already set up for you online, you will need to do very little preparation. However, it would be good to spend some time running through the more basic coding tutorials. None is exceedingly difficult, but because it's possible to work through them to anticipate hiccups, it's a good idea to do so.
- Have teens choose a project from those highlighted at http://code.org.
- Go forth and have fun!
- Reward each teen who earns a completion certificate with a small prize. Ask teens, particularly those who are new to you, to come to your Technology Makers program. This is your demographic right here!

RESOURCES

Hour of Code: http://hourofcode.com/us
Made w/ Code: www.madewithcode.com
Code Academy: www.codecademy.org

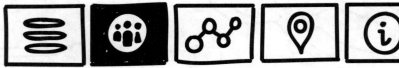

→ Tiny Targets

Who doesn't love projectiles? This program allows teens to improve their game of folded paper, finger flick football, and paper airplanes with miniature versions of catapults, archery bows, and others. Using low-cost materials, teens will be forced to use their ingenuity to re-create and improve designs for their projectile projects.

SHOPPING LIST

- Tape measure

A Variety of Building Supplies such as
- Bamboo grill skewers
- Cotton swabs (can also be used as arrows)
- Craft sticks (notched or plain)
- Cardboard
- Paper
- Cardboard tubes
- Plastic bottles

A Variety of Connecting Supplies such as
- Rubber bands
- Duct tape
- String
- Hot glue guns or other fast-drying glue

A Variety of Projectiles such as
- Bouncy balls
- Pom-poms
- Buttons

MAKE IT HAPPEN

- Print out schematics for such projectile tools as catapults, trebuchets, slingshots, and others (see Resources).
- Print or draw some targets and place them in your testing area.
- Provide teens with the materials and encourage them to work either in teams or individually to create something to throw something.
- Set a time for the first test. Measure how far each projectile goes.
- Have teens revise designs and test again!

RESOURCES

Austin, John. *Mini Weapons of Mass Destruction: Build Implements of Spitball Warfare.* Chicago Review Press, 2009.

Make It @ Your Library—DIY Viking Catapult: http://makeitatyourlibrary.org/outside-play/ diy-viking-catapult-bamboo-skewers#.VHdQ5PTF_b0

◘ Learn to Solder

If teens intend to get into electronics work, robotics, or other tech-making projects, soldering will be a handy skill to have. This program introduces teens to the basics and gives them a chance to practice this skill. Many varieties of learn-to-solder kits are on the market in the $10–$15 range. If correctly assembled, these kits will give teens the chance to learn how to solder and wind up with a functioning electronics project at the end.

Two or even three teens could work together on one kit if you are conserving funds. If the cost of individual kits may make this a difficult program to host, call on your community to help out. Reach out to ham radio operators in your area or contact any local branches or the outreach coordinator of ARRL (American Radio Relay League). An old ham worth his or her salt will have at the ready a "junk box" with lots of printed circuit boards (PCBs) and electronics parts to play on and will likely be thrilled to hear about young people who are eager to learn about this technology.

If you haven't done it before, soldering is akin to using a hot glue gun to attach seed beads to a credit card—but with metal. Consider the temperament and cautiousness of your group before attempting this project. It's definitely doable, but you know your teens best, and you'll know when they're ready for it.

CROSSOVER

- Scientific Teens

SHOPPING LIST

- Safety glasses
- Learn-to-solder kits (available from a wide variety of vendors online and at hobby shops)
  or
- Junked printed circuit boards or blank perfboard that can be cut to size
- A collection of LEDs, resistors, capacitors, and other electronics parts
- Solder
- Soldering irons
- Flux
- Small piece of sponge or paper towel (damp)

MAKE IT HAPPEN

- You will want to try this activity yourself before assisting teens. Plan an afternoon to play with the tools and get a feel for what teens will be doing in your program.
- To safely prepare your space, follow the instructions with your kit or those found here: www.dummies.com/how-to/content/safe-soldering-checklist.html.
- Print out keys to translate schematic diagrams for teens if they are using a kit. This is how they will know which piece to connect in which spot.
- Show teens how to start soldering. Circulate around the room and keep an eye out in particular for any breaches in safety.
- Refer to YouTube videos for expert techniques and strategies.

RESOURCES

Electrical Symbols and Electronic Symbols: www.rapidtables.com/electric/electrical _symbols.htm

SparkFun Electronics—How to Solder: https://learn.sparkfun.com/tutorials/how-to-solder ---through-hole-soldering

⬒ Introduction to Computer Animation

It is a natural progression from watching lots of animated movies and television to creating your own. Teens will learn the basics of the free Pencil2D program with the help of online tutorials at sessions at the library. Teens who are familiar with the program can mentor the others and offer basic tips at this interactive event.

SHOPPING LIST

- Laptops: Teens will need access to laptops loaded with Pencil2D (www.pencil2d.org/pencil2d/)
- Drawing pad: Use of a drawing pad for computers is not necessary, but teens may enjoy trying techniques with that as well.
- Jump drive: Teens may want to save their work at the end of the session.

MAKE IT HAPPEN

- Pencil2D is an easy-to-use, layered system of creating simple, computer-drawn animation. You will want to familiarize yourself with the program before the session, as well as discover which teens have already used it. This very basic tutorial is a good start, though others exist: www.youtube.com/watch?v=zuW7vWianJM.
- When teens have all arrived, take them through the first few frames of the first layer, with help from teens who are familiar with the program. You could also project the tutorials for this session.
- Learning Pencil2D takes time, and teens may complete only a few frames of different layers during the session.
- When time is up, teens may choose to save their projects to work on at their next visit to the library. You can collect the files and e-mail them to teens or have the files available for future use.

VARIATIONS

- Animation Contest: Teens can submit Pencil2D animation projects for a contest, with the clips to be shown at a future meeting of this club.

ONLINE

- Pencil2D Tutorials: Club members can design their own Pencil2D Animation Tutorials that will be displayed on the library website.

⊡ Stop Motion Animation

Part film festival, part hands-on workshop, this session will look at claymation and LEGO stop motion animation to show teens what is involved in making those movies.

SHOPPING LIST

- Teens in groups will need an iPad loaded with Boinx iStopMotion for iPad animation and iStop camera. Other software exists for Macs especially, and the type of software is optional. This is a fast and inexpensive way to introduce teens to beginning stop motion animation.
- LEGOs (buildings, people, vehicles to make movies)

MAKE IT HAPPEN

- Show several claymation short movies at the club, such as Wallace and Gromit or Gumby. This may be fun to do at Oscar time when some animated nominees may be claymation.
- Show some online clips of Brickfilms or LEGO stop motion creations.
- Show a tutorial in stop motion animation with the iPads and set up teens in groups with props and iPads to begin taking photos and editing. Several exist, but this one (after a short advertisement) has good, basic information with the iPad: www.youtube.com/watch?v = kiCj2HT92PM. (*Note*: Some comments have bad language; adjust the screen to show just the movie when projecting.)
- This project may likely take a few sessions or a longer meeting, but teens should be able to produce a basic movie quickly. Some may be familiar with this process already.

VARIATIONS

- Brickfilm Contest: Invite teens to pull LEGOs out of their closets and make some simple movies. Claymation or other toy movies are also an option, but LEGO movies are likely the easiest to make. Consider allowing teens time with the iPads in the library to work on their entries.
- Claymation: Provide Sculpey and have teens design figures during the meeting. To film at the next meeting, these figures will need to be baked in between meetings, but teens will enjoy seeing what is involved in making these kinds of figures.

ONLINE

- Post links to tutorials on short movies and provide a list of claymation DVDs owned by the library, especially those featuring Wallace and Gromit or Gumby.

RESOURCES

Claymation and Stop Motion in the Classroom: https://sites.google.com/site/movies2bmade/home
Stop Motion Central (for more information on Brickfilms and tips on shooting):
www.stopmotioncentral.com

Traveling Teens

Technology allows teens to travel virtually and experience other cultures even if they are not physically able to do so. The travel club need not be teens who are able to go elsewhere, but ones who might like to, or who just want to learn about other lands. This club can cross over ideas from several others, such as the Read-a-Latte Books and Media Club, where instead of focusing on nonfiction generally, teens can look at travel materials from the library or fiction set in different cultures.

POWER PROMOTION

- Promotional materials for this club should emphasize that teens will not have to be travelers themselves to join, just that they may want to learn about other places.
- In the teen area, create a mini trivia game with posters of recognizable landmarks in Paris, Rome, London, Egypt, and other familiar places and offer a prize to teens who can identify all the places pictured.
- Give teens who attend meetings of this group a passport and stamp or sticker attendance each month. Offer prizes for attending every three or more meetings to keep momentum going.

CROSSOVER PROGRAMS

- Ancient Fashions—Fashionista Teens
- Best. Trip. Ever. Scrapbook—Scrapbooking and Photography
- Spice It Up!—Food Fans
- Teens Get Real with Reading—Read-a-Latte Books and Media Club (focus on travel nonfiction or fiction set in different cultures)

➡ Safety and Saving Tips for Travel

Though useful for adults too, this session will focus on ways teens can stay safe and save money when traveling. For many teens who are currently not in a position to do much actual traveling, this program will give them a lot to think about and help them feel more comfortable and confident once the opportunity arises.

SHOPPING LIST

- Props for packing (These include a carry-on–sized suitcase and items such as clothes and toiletries. Items that teens may want but that won't fit should be included so they have to make choices when packing.)

MAKE IT HAPPEN

Airplane Fun: Airplane travel is expensive and often uncomfortable these days. Have teens compare prices for flights on dates at holiday, winter, and summer times to a desired location. How much is first class? How much do teens think food is on the flight? Then have teens look up flights on Expedia and other discount travel sites. Show teens how to put an alert on flight destinations to find a good price, and discuss good times to travel.

Packing Savvy: Bring a rolling carry-on suitcase and several changes of clothes, books, toiletries, and more and have teens choose what should go in, what to leave (fancy hair devices), and how best to pack to get through airport security quickly. Have teens develop their own must-have list, including medications, chargers, books, and more to see what they really need. Show teens how paying for luggage can add up. Can a family or group use one big suitcase and pay for it? What other packing strategies can they think of?

Trains—Really? Train travel is a necessity in Europe, and teens should also know about managing the subway system in cities such as Boston and Washington, D.C. Show maps for a popular city and help teens figure out how to travel from point A to point B quickly. Also look at train travel and costs from a nearby city to a travel destination for comparison to airfare.

Finding the Offbeat and Good Treats: Show teens travel guides such as *Lonely Planet* and restaurant guides to help find cheaper and more unique sightseeing. Many big restaurants have less-expensive carryout menus or attached bakeries so travelers can enjoy the flavors without the service costs. Discuss how teens can find inexpensive meals while traveling.

Being a Tourist at Home: No money for a vacation? Teens can use the same travel guides and research a city or town within driving distance to find something new or to locate unique restaurants. Is there something teens have always wanted to do or a place they haven't visited since a grade school field trip? Time to go back. If possible, take teens on a guided tour by boat or bus and encourage them to learn more about your state and local cities. Try a cemetery tour or a chocolate tour.

Taxis and Tipping: When and how much should teens tip? Discuss calculating rates and tipping hotel staff.

Safety: Discuss hotel safety tips, such as locking room and balcony doors, putting chairs under doorknobs, not saying credit card numbers or other personal information loudly in the room, and other measures. What information should be given to friendly co-travelers? Have teens come up with ways to keep money and valuables safe, and discuss what to do if ID and credit cards are stolen in different cities or countries. Who can teens ask about safe areas near hotels or tourist attractions? Discuss how to find this information either with ratings or through hotel staff. Youth hostels are another option for some locations, and they have unique rules. Find one in a nearby city online and go over its rules to show teens the realities of hosteling as well as the advantages.

VARIATIONS

- Rather than use props, give teens a list of items with approximate weight and a limit to fit into a suitcase and have them figure it out on paper.
- Amazing Race: Have teens figure out the least expensive way to get from Orlando to Seattle in December under two days.
- Dream Vacations: Teens can look up information on traveling to their dream destination for ten days and staying in a luxury resort.

ONLINE

- Any of the topics other than packing could transfer to an online article with links, such as interesting destinations at a nearby city.

RESOURCES

Teen Travel Talk: www.teentraveltalk.com

⮕ Study Abroad

Some teens may take study abroad programs into consideration when selecting a college. This session discusses options for studying abroad and ways teens can find more information.

MAKE IT HAPPEN

Guest Speakers: This program works best with guest speakers if possible. Invite representatives from colleges with study abroad programs or students who have been through those programs to talk about the experience and how it can enhance college opportunities.

Options: Teens can take intensive language programs abroad, volunteer, or spend time studying around the world. What are ways to begin the process at home? Local colleges may offer short trips and language and culture classes to give teens a feel for a particular country.

International Careers: Help teens identify ways particular countries or connections to international businesses would enhance their chosen career to help them narrow down programs. For example, a teen who wants to teach Spanish may want to spend time in Spain or Mexico and would then look at colleges with those programs. A teen who wants to design technology may find opportunities to study in Japan and learn that language. Once teens look at their choices, research becomes easier.

VARIATIONS

- Host a contest in which teens write a fictional story about an exchange student and have to incorporate details of the culture and location. Traveling Teens can act as judges, and winners can be awarded a gift certificate to a local international cuisine restaurant (depending on availability).

ONLINE

- Post a list of fiction and nonfiction titles about foreign study or exchange students. Be sure to highlight titles that address both the fun and exploration aspects and the culture clashes and realistic challenges.

RESOURCES

The Princeton Review—College Study Abroad Programs: www.princetonreview.com/college-study-abroad-programs.aspx

→ Learning Languages at the Library

Can teens learn a new language at the library? At the end of this session, teens will be able to say some basic phrases ("I want a book" is a good one) in several languages.

SHOPPING LIST

- Snacks (optional; provide Chinese, Mexican, Indian, Italian, or other foods from a local restaurant for teens to enjoy while learning some new words)

MAKE IT HAPPEN

- Pull language CDs or DVDs from the library collection in several different languages. If available, project a computer tied in to the library database on languages. Spend at least ten minutes on each language, learning some basic phrases. Teens may help choose languages.
- Multilingual Teens: Ask club members who speak another language to teach the group some appropriate phrases.
- Take teens on a tour of the library, both virtually and physically, to show them where to find materials for learning to speak and read another language. Instruct them on how to access any databases from home and show how those work.

ONLINE

- Make navigating databases easy for teens by putting up screenshots directing them on how to use the online databases on languages.

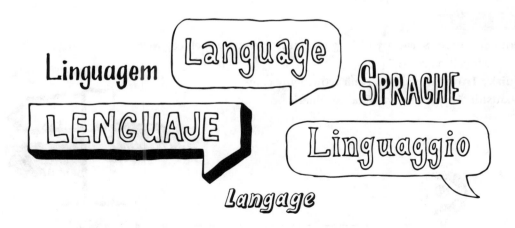

→ Quirky Local Secrets

Every community or region has its own quirks, secrets, historical curiosities, and local color. This program encourages teens to combine their collective knowledge to create a quirky local guidebook for each other or to share with a wider audience.

SHOPPING LIST

- Nothing is needed, but if there's a favorite local food spot that might work into your conversation, pick up some snacks to share!

MAKE IT HAPPEN

- Pull books and sites together that highlight unusual sightseeing spots, extra fun restaurants, and places not to be missed. See the Resources section for ideas.
- Brainstorm all the insider knowledge that the teens have about your community.
- Sort their tidbits into categories: places to go, things to do, what to eat, great shopping spots, local color, and so on.
- Have teens form groups to flesh out the various categories, adding addresses, hours of operation, tips, and narratives about what makes these spots special.
- Publish the teens' compiled work! This can be a low-tech zine style using a photocopier, an e-book that is freely available to download from the library's website, or a web-based magazine. Partner with the Scrapbooking and Photography Club to add photos.

VARIATIONS

- Work with Technology Makers to convert the collected information into an app or a mobile-friendly web page.

RESOURCES

Oddball Travel Series by Chicago Review Press: www.chicagoreviewpress.com/oddball-pages-487.php
Quirky Travel Guy: http://quirkytravelguy.com
Roadside America: www.roadsideamerica.com

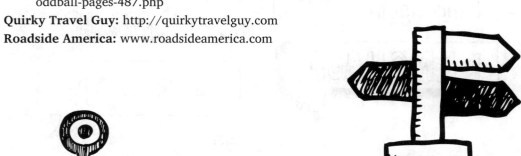

➡ Travel App Showdown

There's an app for everything these days. Especially for travelers, smartphone and tablet apps can be great for planning routes, finding cool spots, and connecting with people and activities. This program highlights teens' favorite apps and puts them in the driver's seat.

MAKE IT HAPPEN

- Ahead of this meeting, encourage teens to think about their favorite apps for travel.
- On the day of the meeting, set up a projector to allow projecting phone and tablet screens, either via Bluetooth or with cords.
- Have teens take turns demonstrating and talking about their favorite travel apps. It may be helpful to sort the apps into different categories: wayfinding, activities, connecting with people, weather, location-specific apps.
- Consider some of the following apps to demonstrate:
  - Geocaching—a scavenger hunt all over the world!
  - iStone—language translation
  - Postagram—mails your travel photos as postcards
  - Waze—social mapping
  - Wikitude—augmented reality for recommended sites

→ Armchair Traveler Movie Nights

For teens with a yen for adventure but not much opportunity to travel, host a series of movie nights to highlight the fabulous world beyond your local boundaries. Choose a mix of documentaries and feature films to help teens see the realities of life abroad as well as get lost in some good stories. This makes a nice after-hours event and could easily be turned into a movie marathon day depending on the needs and interests of club members.

CROSSOVER

- Read-a-Latte Books and Media Club

SHOPPING LIST

- Projector and screen
- Movie with public performance rights
- Refreshments

MAKE IT HAPPEN

- Obtain the public performance rights to the film you intend to show.
    - Look into individual or blanket movie licensing at Swank (www.movlic.com).
    - Explore the offerings through PBS's documentary series *Independent Lens* (www.pbs.org/independentlens), which offers real-time Internet screenings followed by discussions.
    - Consider a subscription to Film Movement (www.filmmovement.com), which offers foreign and independent films with public performance rights pricing.
- Consider promoting this event with other local groups: film societies, foreign exchange student or cultural exploration groups, or foreign language conversation clubs.
- Introduce the movie, or encourage a teen to introduce the movie, and enjoy!

VARIATIONS

- Run a film festival contest in which teens submit and then view movies on a travel theme.
- Focus on one region at a time, or travel around the world, using a prominently displayed map to track your route.
- Host a MuVChat (www.muvchat.com) to encourage participation via texting during the screening.
- If public performance rights are cost prohibitive for your group, run this as a self-directed program by providing a list of movies for teens to check out and watch at home, then gather to discuss—with popcorn, of course!

➡ Travel Vision Board

By browsing websites, magazines, and ads and selecting words and ideas, teens can bring together a collection that appeals to them, and in doing so, begin to define their own travel dreams and goals. The result can be a physical piece created on poster board, a notebook that can be pulled out of a purse and added to on the fly, or a digital board created on Pinterest, Polyvore, or Tumblr.

CROSSOVER

- Strike the word *travel* and the vision board concept can be applied to any other club as a way for teens to clarify their interests and dream big.

SHOPPING LIST

- Travel magazines, Sunday newspaper Travel sections, and other print media
- Quotation books
- Computers, tablets, or laptops with Internet access
- Poster board
- Scissors
- Glue sticks

MAKE IT HAPPEN

- First encourage teens to browse for quotations and phrases, either in books or online, that they identify with. These quotes and phrases don't need to relate directly to travel; they should just be ideas that light a spark.
- Have teens also browse for images—either of landmarks, scenes, travel gear, or other types of design (buildings, cars, nature themes, famous artworks)—that similarly spark a response.
- Invite teens to collect the words and images into a collage—either online or on the poster board. Encourage teens to notice patterns and group items in an aesthetically pleasing way.
- Have teens take a step back and analyze the boards. Talk about them as a group. Help teens to think about trends that they see in each individual board. Do they see more green space or more urban settings? Are specific cultures or countries dominant? Does a theme (music, history, ecotourism, light travel, social activism) or feeling (dreaminess, joyfulness, personal discovery, extreme travel) emerge when teens take all the pieces into account?
- Invite teens to write about what they have learned about their personal travel style and aspirations from the exercise.

ONLINE

■ This activity can be done exclusively online, either with websites designed for collaging or by creating your own collage and uploading it.

RESOURCES

5 Ideas to Create Your Vision Board: www.stylebizarre.com/2014/01/vision-board-ideas.html

4 Steps to Creating an Online Travel Vision Board: http://happyblackwoman.com/4-steps-to-creating-an-online-travel-vision-board

How to Make a Vision Board: www.wikihow.com/Make-a-Vision-Board

More Ideas for Established Clubs

In *A Year* of *Programs for Teens* and *A Year of Programs for Teens 2*, the authors discussed several clubs and listed activities for each. In this chapter, updates and further activities for many of those groups are presented, using programs from clubs listed in previous chapters in this book.

Teen Advisory Boards

Still a cornerstone of teen programming, the Teen Advisory Board (TAB) can direct and inspire all other events and services. Many activities listed for other clubs could transfer to a TAB meeting. Testing them out on the established group can be a good way to gauge interest or launch a new club.

Having an online and paper application form can actually be good advertising for a Teen Advisory Board. Asking a few questions about why teens want to volunteer for the library and what they like best about it helps avoid a situation in which parents are forcing teens to attend. Invite teens to list skills and contact information as well as birthdays. The form will help teens see what may be involved with the TAB and get them invested in the group. Prospective TAB members should be reassured that no one is rejected from the group and that the form is simply a means of gathering information.

Few can resist exclusive events. Advertise some events in the library newsletter that are for TAB members only, and other teens who want to come need only fill out an application for the TAB. These events need not be huge undertakings, but they could have a higher planning cost, require a little more assistance, or offer some extra appeal: a popular guest speaker, door prizes, or a tie-in to a hot topic. These special events will be attractive enough to keep your current teens engaged and encourage new membership.

Crossover programs from this book that would work especially well and have general appeal for Teen Advisory Board meetings include the following:

- Crafting for Charity (any of the themes would work for a TAB; Color a Smile is a good, basic activity to start with)
- Photo and Video Blogs—Newsworthy Teens
- Extreme Gingerbread—Food Fans
- Teen Tasters—Food Fans
- Geocaching—Scientific Teens
- Forensic Fun—Scientific Teens
- Self-Defense Basics—Active Teens
- Library Garden—Active Teens
- Decades of Dance Moves—Active Teens
- Recycling Challenge—Green Teens
- Flea Market—Green Teens
- Stop Motion Animation—Technology Makers

Teen Writing Clubs

Creative teens will always be looking for an outlet at the library, and the writing club can be another place to launch other clubs, especially for those teens who want to create anime stories or act out skits. Given new opportunities to publish with technology, teens may be interested in trying new techniques, formats, and ways to publish and promote their work.

Crossover programs from clubs that may work especially well for Teen Writing Clubs include the following:

- Photo and Video Blogs—Newsworthy Teens
- Just One Sentence Journaling—Scrapbooking and Photography
- Promoting Yourself—Newsworthy Teens
- Cartoon Capers—Newsworthy Teens
- So Bad, It's Good Poetry Slam—Entertaining Teens
- Stop Motion Animation—Technology Makers

CREATEens

Many teens like to make crafts, gifts, and art objects to wear and express their style. CREATEens introduces teens to new media and techniques for projects.

Crossover programs from clubs that may inspire the CREATEens group include these:

- Polymer Food Charms—Fashionista Teens
- Apron Decoration—Fashionista Teens
- Retro Fashions—Fashionista Teens
- Ancient Fashions—Fashionista Teens
- Simple Scarves—Fashionista Teens
- Trashion Show—Fashionista Teens
- Recipe Scrapbooking—Scrapbooking and Photography
- Quilled Cards—Scrapbooking and Photography
- Mini Photo Books—Scrapbooking and Photography
- Crafting for Charity (any program described for this club would work with a crafty club)
- Garden Art—Green Teens
- Rain Barrel Decoration—Green Teens
- Forcing Potted Bulbs—Green Teens

Volunteering and Community Service

Always appealing to this generation of teens, this club will continue to serve others in the community and beyond. Many programs written for clubs in this book lend themselves well to a club with a service theme, including these:

- Crafting for Charity (any program described for this club would fulfill the service club mission; see also the Crossover Programs section in that chapter)
- Recycling Challenge—Green Teens
- Flea Market—Green Teens

Money Mavericks

This club was designed to teach teens to be money smart and inspire them to earn and save money toward their futures.

Crossover programs from clubs that may also appeal to Money Mavericks include the following:

- Promoting Yourself—Newsworthy Teens
- Safety and Saving Tips for Travel—Traveling Teens
- Making Money from Entertainment—Entertaining Teens
- Flea Market—Green Teens

Techno Teens

Techno Teens will always enjoy learning new programs or skills with technology. Many programs list online variations that the Techno Teens may enjoy especially, but several programs also lend themselves well to Techno Teens meetings, including the following:

- Photo and Video Blogs—Newsworthy Teens
- Phone Photography or Movie Contest—Scrapbooking and Photography
- Paranormal Science?—Scientific Teens
- Forensic Fun—Scientific Teens
- Geocaching—Scientific Teens
- Technology Makers (any of the programs would work)

Drama Dynamics

Teens may not have access to strong drama programs in their schools or time available to be in plays even if they have an interest in doing so. Let teens try out drama on a smaller scale with this club. Several programs described in this book would work for a drama club too, including the following:

- Photo and Video Blogs—Newsworthy Teens
- Phone Photography or Movie Contest—Scrapbooking and Photography
- Promoting Yourself—Newsworthy Teens
- Entertaining Teens (any of the programs would likely appeal to drama-focused teens, too)
- Stop Motion Animation—Technology Makers

Telling Stories with Film

Technology has made filming and editing easier even since *A Year of Programs for Teens 2* was published, and several programs described in this book will also appeal to a film-inspired group:

- Mad about Music and Movies—Read-a-Latte Books and Media Club
- Ancient Fashions—Fashionista Teens (for costuming purposes)
- Trashion Show—Fashionista Teens (for costuming purposes)
- Photo and Video Blogs—Newsworthy Teens
- Phone Photography or Movie Contest—Scrapbooking and Photography
- Promoting Yourself—Newsworthy Teens
- Taking the Fear Out of Public Speaking—Entertaining Teens
- Stop Motion Animation—Technology Makers

INDEX